Conversations About History
Volume 1

Conversations About

HISTORY

Volume 1

Edited by Howard Burton

Ideas Roadshow conversations present a wealth of candid insights from some of the world's leading experts, generated through a focused yet informal setting. They are explicitly designed to give non-specialists a uniquely accessible window into frontline research and scholarship that wouldn't otherwise be encountered through standard lectures and textbooks.

Over 100 Ideas Roadshow conversations have been held since our debut in 2012, covering a wide array of topics across the arts and sciences.

All Ideas Roadshow conversations are available both as part of a collection or as an individual eBook.

See www.ideasroadshow.com for a full listing of all titles.

Copyright ©2021 Open Agenda Publishing. All rights reserved.

ISBN: 978-1-77170-101-3 (pb)
ISBN: 978-1-77170-102-0 (eBook)

Edited, with preface and all introductions written by Howard Burton.

All *Ideas Roadshow Conversations* use Canadian spelling.

Contents

TEXTUAL NOTE 7

PREFACE 9

ENLIGHTENED ENTREPRENEURIALISM
A CONVERSATION WITH MARGARET JACOB

    Introduction 17
    I. Historical Origins 22
    II. Decrypting Newton 27
    III. Beyond the Numbers 30
    IV. Apprenticeship 37
    V. Religion and Geography 40
    VI. Theory vs. Practice 44
    VII. Lessons Learned? 47
    VIII. History Today 51
    IX. Past and Future 55
    X. Righting Wrongs, Slowly 59
    Continuing the Conversation 63

SCIENCE AND PSEUDOSCIENCE
A CONVERSATION WITH MICHAEL GORDIN

    Introduction 67
    I. A Counterculture Hero 73
    II. An Ideal Case 78
    III. The Lysenko Lesson 82
    IV. A Freudian Cosmology 88
    V. Enter Einstein 92
    VI. Responses and Reactions 96
    VII. Digging In 101
    VIII. Science vs. Pseudoscience 105
    IX. Fringe Benefits 112
    X. Learning From History 116
    XI. Anthropic Digression 123
    XII. Better Science? 128
    Continuing the Conversation 133

THE CONSOLATIONS OF HISTORY
A CONVERSATION WITH TEOFILO RUIZ

Introduction 137
I. The Terror of History 142
II. Becoming a Historian 148
III. Historical Ruminations 161
IV. Progress? 171
V. Connecting 179
VI. Looking Ahead 186
Continuing the Conversation 194

HERCULANEUM UNCOVERED
A CONVERSATION WITH ANDREW WALLACE-HADRILL

Introduction 197
I. What We Know 202
II. Letting Sleeping Dogs Lie 211
III. Exploring Roman Society 215
IV. Herculaneum vs. Pompeii 223
V. The Future of the Past 228
Continuing the Conversation 239

EMBRACING COMPLEXITY
A CONVERSATION WITH DAVID CANNADINE

Introduction 243
I. Finding One's Historical Feet 248
II. The Art of Biography 254
III. The Undivided Past 261
IV. Transcending Parochialism 266
V. Categorical Examinations 271
VI. Historical Broadening 277
VII. What to Do, Part I 282
VIII. What to Do, Part II 286
Continuing the Conversation 292

Textual Note

The contents of this book are based upon separate filmed conversations with Howard Burton and each of the five featured experts.

Margaret Jacob is Distinguished Professor of History at UCLA. This conversation occurred on September 21, 2014.

Michael Gordin is Rosengarten Professor of Modern and Contemporary History at Princeton University. This conversation occurred on June 7, 2014.

Teofilo Ruiz is Professor Emeritus of History at UCLA. This conversation occurred on April 4, 2014.

Andrew Wallace-Hadrill is Director of Research and Honorary Professor of Roman Studies in the Faculty of Classics at the University of Cambridge. This conversation occurred on March 22, 2013.

David Cannadine is the Dodge Professor of History at Princeton University and the editor of the Oxford Dictionary of National Biography. This conversation occurred on October 21, 2014.

Howard Burton is the creator and host of Ideas Roadshow and was Founding Executive Director of Perimeter Institute for Theoretical Physics.

Preface

Many people like to throw around the phrase "the lessons of history", but a moment's reflection reveals how problematic such a notion actually is. Which lessons? Drawn by whom, exactly? For what purpose?

Indeed, the one thing any serious student of history quickly appreciates is that the naive view of history as a steady cascade of objectively verifiable events is, well, very naive. That's not to say, of course, that we can never distinguish between what actually happened and what didn't, but even the very notion of "what happened" tends to involve a wide variety of opinions depending on whose perspective you consider, let alone what might be responsible for events occurring in the first place.

Of course it needs to be appreciated that the rush to simplify our understanding, to fit our sense of the past into a tightly boxed, pre-set narrative, is all too human; and even professional historians are hardly immune to it. But genuine historical understanding inevitably springs from going beyond any one all-encompassing picture to appreciate that details that *don't* fit in with our explanatory structure are often just as significant than those that do—indeed, sometimes even more so.

This collection contains many examples of the importance of recognizing the manifold, full-bodied complexities inherent in any sophisticated treatment of history. UCLA historian of science **Margaret Jacob** explicitly calls for an inherently multi-disciplinary, nuanced approach to historical events rather than looking for one explanatory silver bullet to interpret all past trajectories—a tendency, she notes disapprovingly, that economic historians seem particularly partial to.

> "I think it's wrong to separate science and manual labour, I think they belong together. I can show John Marshall in his Leeds textile factory trying to apply Newtonian principles to the operation of bobbins and to the problem of friction. In my opinion, then, it's wrong to see all of this as separated. We are the ones, our sociology, that creates 'The History of Science', 'The History of Technology', 'The History of Music' and so forth, but that's not the way that human beings actually experience the world.

> "I think the statue has cracked now, and there are economic historians who are increasingly concerned with culture, trying to figure out how you fit cultural explanations into this phenomenon of industrial development. What still prevails, I would say, among the majority of practitioners of economic history, is a desire to find the single, sufficient cause. Whether it's abundant coal, high wages, semi-literate tinkerers, there's a sense that, There's got to be one thing that really causes this; and I think that's a very flawed way of doing history.

> "Now, people may turn around and say, 'Well, you're saying that science is the one key. But what I'm really saying is that it's just **one** key. You can't understand what happens on the ground unless you look at these people as thinking entrepreneurs and capitalists who are trying to work out problems. They're bringing to bear the knowledge that they've learned in school, in private study groups, in scientific societies, and all kinds of places. If you leave that out of the story, you impoverish it."

Then there are the trenchant insights of Princeton University historian of science **Michael Gordin**, who cautions us to recognize that the much-trumpeted Popperian criterion of falsifiability that is frequently invoked to distinguish science from "pseudoscience" is far less straightforward than most of its proponents typically appreciate.

> "I often get this quoted to me by undergraduates who don't see why I'm so exercised about this question of demarcation. They say, 'Look, it's simple: falsifiability.' It's a very appealing criterion. Except it's got a couple of problems.

> "The first problem is, How do you know that you falsified something? If it were the case that every time an experiment with a null result meant that you'd falsified something, then everything we know about physics and chemistry will be wrong because high school students around the world have failed to replicate it. So you have to do the experiment right.
>
> "But how do you know you've done the experiment 'right', unless you get 'the right result'? This is something sociologists call 'the experimenter's regress': you really need to figure out some way of breaking that cycle. How do you know you've done the experiment right but gotten a null result? So that's one particular problem that can be very, very touchy in lots of cases."

UCLA medievalist **Teofilo Ruiz**, meanwhile, points out that even dry administrative documents are often replete with all manner of historical subtleties when viewed by those who live hundreds of years later.

> "When I first began doing scholarly research, I'd look at a document in the municipal archive of Burgos. But now let's dig deeper into that: Who wrote those documents? For what purpose are these documents written? These documents that allow us to see that the past is also mediated by such things as basic literary skills, for example, in a society where the majority of people are illiterate.
>
> "Most of these documents are either administrative documents or having to do with transfers of property. They provide, shall we say, a written garment to something very specific, which is the nature of owning things, of relationships of power, of social distinctions and so on. How are we to see the past objectively, when the material that allows us to see the past is necessarily clouded by these structures?
>
> "This is the great challenge that postmodern theory posed for historians: If language is unstable, how could you know anything that happened? As a historian, I say, 'No, no. There is something you can know.' But no well-trained historian today will look at the past in the same fashion that we did 30 years ago. We will be more critical of our sources, we will try to find alternate points of views, and so forth."

And then there are the deeply counterintuitive insights by University of Cambridge archaeologist **Andrew Wallace-Hadrill**, who confronts us with the thought that even the very motivation to examine the past is often a product of contemporary societal forces.

> *"The second moment of revelation for me was when I was visiting Pozzuoli, which is on the north of the Bay of Naples. Pozzuoli suffered from dreadful earthquakes in 1980 and the whole historic centre had to be abandoned—it was in such terrible condition. There's a wonderful cathedral there, which is built in the remains of an ancient temple, and you can see the columns of the temple. In fact the earthquake actually helped us, because it "shook down" a lot of the Baroque decoration and made the Roman columns smile through.*
>
> *"So it's a really fascinating site; and after the earthquake it became possible to do excavations. And it emerged that there is a 17th-century city built on top of the abandoned and backfilled remains of the earlier medieval city that extended back to ancient times. Not surprisingly, the excavators found quite a lot of statues: Puteoli was a major Roman city, so naturally there were loads of statues. But the odd thing that they spotted was that the statues had been deliberately abandoned there in the process of backfilling the site in order to build the new city on top. That is to say, the people who backfilled it knew that they were throwing away ancient statues.*
>
> *"And I was really struck by that, because then I thought, Ah. The interesting question isn't so much, Why do people excavate and look for the past? but, When do they **not** want to find the past? And suddenly, you see, you've got to explain **why** they want it. It's not obvious that people want to discover the past. They want to discover the past because it's useful to them."*

Our final example of the need to embrace the complexities of history comes from Princeton University historian **David Cannadine**, one of the most passionate and insightful advocates imaginable for the need to regularly transcend standard historical categorizations, as detailed in his book, *The Undivided Past*.

"It's certainly the case that one of the motivations behind writing The Undivided Past was to put forward the argument that the constant invitation to see the world in terms of these warring collectivities who are, as it were, predestined to exist and to fight, is not the whole of the human story; and we deeply misunderstand the human story if we don't understand that.

"Beyond that, when politicians and pundits and false profits stand up and say to us, 'The world is very simple, and I will tell you how simple it is and all we need to do to fix it,' it seems to me that it's constantly the job of the historian to say in reply, 'No, the world is very complicated; and you disregard that complication, not only at your peril but probably at ours as well.' And part of the purpose of The Undivided Past was to say, the world may have, on occasions, been built around simple animosities, but much of the time it wasn't and we need to understand that.

"More broadly still than that, I think that the purpose of studying history, the purpose of writing history, and the purpose of reading history, is indeed to try to get ourselves outside ourselves. It seems to me that history is the most powerful antidote to the geographical parochialism—which assumes the only place is here—and the temporal parochialism, which assumes the only time is now. Well, actually, an awful lot of people are living lives now very different from ours in other parts of the world and we ought to take notice of that. And, actually, most of humanity has had very different assumptions about how to live their lives than we have now.

"I think that one of the purposes of historians is to try to explain how other people in other places or other times may have had views which we now find completely unacceptable, but that they weren't necessarily any less decent than we are. So, history is a huge antidote to parochialism. And, with respect to The Undivided Past, one of the parochialisms that I'm targeting in that book is the parochialism that assumes that the way to understand all of the world is through these simple Manichean, binary, antagonistic categories, which seems to me simply not good enough."

My conversation with David, not coincidentally, is called *Embracing Complexity*. But it's safe to say that the very same title could easily apply to any of the other four conversations in this collection.

Enlightened Entrepreneurialism

A conversation with Margaret Jacob

Introduction
Measuring Motivations

An economist, it is said, is someone who can predict the past with unerring accuracy. Historians, meanwhile, set their sights a little higher, trying to shed light on why, all things considered, the past happened as it did.

Sometimes, when the two join forces in the domain known as "economic history", real insights are produced. But not always.

Margaret Jacob, Distinguished Professor of History at UCLA, has often crossed swords with economic historians throughout her career, but it's certainly not because she diminishes the importance of economic factors towards understanding the past.

In her comprehensive analysis on the history of the Industrial Revolution, she's spent considerable time and effort assessing and interpreting the major economic motivations on the ground, comparing and contrasting daily life experiences in England, France, Belgium and the Netherlands.

So what is the problem here? Why the tension between Prof. Jacob and many economic historians?

Well, in the first place, there is the question of breadth.

For Margaret, a sophisticated understanding of the past naturally involves a composite approach that marries economic motivations with associated cultural factors of educational trends, religious influences and scientific and technological awareness, to name but a few.

It's taken quite some time for many economic historians to come around to this broader way of thinking. For decades, many have adamantly maintained that the Industrial Revolution inexorably resulted from two dominant factors: the high cost of wages that strongly incentivized the development of mechanized manufacturing and the preponderance of local coal that drove the resulting machines.

And while rising numbers of economic historians now seem sensitive to also incorporating the unique cultural and societal factors of 18th-century English life, there is still a long way to go towards a genuine meeting of the minds.

> *"I think the statue has cracked now, and there are economic historians trying to figure out how you fit cultural explanations into this phenomenon of industrial development. What still prevails among the majority of practitioners of economic history, however, is a desire to find **the** single, sufficient cause.*
>
> *"Whether it's abundant coal, high wages, semi-literate tinkerers, there's a sense that, **There's got to be one thing that really causes this**; and I think that's a very flawed way of doing history.*
>
> *"Now, people may turn around and say, 'Well, **you're** saying that science is the key.' But what I'm really saying is that it's just **one** key. You can't understand what happens on the ground unless you look at these people as thinking entrepreneurs and capitalists who are trying to work out problems. They're bringing to bear the knowledge that they've learned in school, in private study groups, in scientific societies, and all kinds of places. If you leave that out of the story, you impoverish it."*

As it happens, a closer examination of the data seems to reveal even more differences between the two approaches, even if one does limit oneself strictly to economic factors.

In the first place, Margaret told me, it's not completely true that the cost of wages in England were uniquely higher than anywhere else. Wages in the Dutch Republic at the dawning of the Industrial

Revolution, for example, were *"just as high, if not higher, than those in Britain."*

But her next point is even more telling.

> *"Even if you were to assume that British wages were the highest in the world at the time, these people living and breathing in Britain in the 1770s and 1790s don't know anything about that.*

> *"They're working on the ground with what they've got; and one of the basic principles of economic life is that you always try to minimize your costs wherever you can and increase your profits. This is not rocket science.*

> *"So to say that the high wages in Britain are both distinctive and the motivating factor turns out to be problematic, because they're actually not that distinctive, and this argument of the motivating factor relies upon a more fundamental assumption—which often goes unstated in the economic history literature—that people are "driven by the numbers": they understand immediately that something is "too expensive'"and so they go about finding ways to make it less expensive.*

> *"Well, there's not a lot of evidence for this. If you look at the figures of what's being paid to coal miners in 18th-century Newcastle, nothing's changing: wages were very low and remained low throughout the century.*

> *"What you discover when you really go into a mine, look at the wage structure and see what the engineers say about their expenses, is that the single biggest expense that they keep recording is the cost of horses: **feeding** the horses. Now, the cost of feeding a horse in France versus the cost of feeding a horse in Britain cannot be that different.*

> *"These guys are **not** telling you that what's killing them and their factory is the cost of wages. They're not saying, '**I've got to do everything I can to reduce the labour force, so I'm going to mechanize.**' They're not saying that.*

> *"In order to advance that argument, you have to begin with an assumption that certain things move human beings more than others,*

that they have an instinctive feel for a high-wage setting and will do whatever they have to do to undo that. This is an assumption about the way human beings work that I don't think life experience bears out."

In the end, of course, it comes down to human values: why, as best as we can determine, do people actually do what they do? Oscar Wilde once famously defined a cynic as someone who "knows the price of everything and the value of nothing".

Like most of Wilde's aphorisms, it's not obvious what exactly to make of it, but one point clearly hits home, at least: price and value are not the same thing.

The Conversation

I. Historical Origins
Rebel-turned-scholar

HB: I'd like to begin with some personal questions about your scholarly origins: when you realized that you wanted to be a full-time, professional historian and how that all started for you.

MJ: Well, I went into college wanting to major in science. I came in having done some hydroponic experiments that had won some prizes; and I started off taking freshman chemistry, which is very dull.

I was also taking courses in history and literature and all the usual things at this small, Catholic, women's college in Brooklyn called St. Joseph's, which still exists and is coming up to its hundredth-year anniversary. It's now co-ed and I was recently there for my 50th reunion.

Basically, the courses in history were just so much more interesting than the ones in science. On top of that, I also grew up in a household where Cromwell was alive and well—the ogre of choice, you know?

HB: Were there Irish roots in your family?

MJ: Yes, my mother's from Ireland and she was steeped in Irish Republican history. Her brother was a member of Stormont, The Northern Ireland Parliament, which was totally gerrymandered. Out of 70 seats, I think there were about 11 for Catholics and he had one of those. So history was just part and parcel of our lives. I remember many years later, after I had worked in British history and Dutch history, my mother said to me, *"I wish you'd do the history of your own people!"*

HB: Did you feel any pressure to do that?

MJ: No. I had written a bit on Irish Republicanism in the 18th century, but no, the pressure was not overwhelming. It was just her sense of frustration towards me because I wasn't submerging myself in it.

HB: Well, mothers can never be satisfied, at least not fully.

MJ: Exactly. I own a framed engraving of the first, known pictorial representation of freemasonry—because I worked on free masonry too—that dates back to the 1730s. I remember one Christmas we were having relatives over, and my mother called me up and said, "*Will you please take that picture down. Cousin Rose doesn't want to see the Freemasons on your wall!*" In Northern Ireland, you see, the Masonic Lodges are tied in deeply with the Orange Order, so to her the engraving was deeply offensive. So I took it down.

HB: How long had she been offended by it, you think?

MJ: Probably from the moment I put it up. But she wasn't going to do anything about it until cousin Rose came, and then it was just too much. Some battles you just don't fight. I took it down, they came, and we had a great Christmas. And then I put it right back up.

HB: Getting back to your story, you were at St. Joseph's, bored by your freshman chemistry classes, and so began drifting towards the humanities.

First a personal reaction: Who cares about chemistry? Everybody knows *that's* boring. What about physics? Why not even pure mathematics?

MJ: Well, I certainly did do pure math—I made a living on the side teaching geometry to high school students. But I'm not sure why I never moved over towards the other sciences. I just stayed in chemistry before moving over to history.

I was lucky in that the nuns who taught us history had PhDs from places like Columbia and Yale. They were serious scholars, and the quality of the teaching in history was very high. And then, I guess, luckily I just became good at it quite quickly.

When I went to graduate school, I realized that all of the theology and philosophy that I'd had to take because they were all required courses was actually helpful. I'd hated all that at the time—I joined an underground "cell" at the college and we printed a newspaper called *The Lutheran*.

HB: Really? Wow, you were really quite the rebel.

MJ: Yes, indeed. I was quite alienated, and I stopped being Catholic by my sophomore year. But I stayed on because I had to: there was no other secular education that would accept those credits. I would have lost a year.

HB: Really? Despite those nuns with the PhDs?

MJ: Well, there was all this philosophy and theology that was required, not to mention the two-credit course in Gregorian chant—

HB: Hold on. Back up a minute. You took a credit course in Gregorian chant?

MJ: Yes, it was required.

HB: Can you still do it?

MJ: No, I couldn't do it then. I still remember Father D'Ecclesias, poor man. At the end of the academic year, you had to sing for your exam grade, and I can still see this man listening to me and just feeling so badly for him and what he must have been feeling.

I mean, it was a slaughter of innocents: sounds that were never meant to be heard in a classroom, let alone a church. It was very difficult material, but even so.

At any rate, all those credits wouldn't translate had I gone to a secular or city college, which meant that I would have lost at least a year, if not more. So I was stuck, as it were, but the other thing was that this was also during Vatican II—it was a time of great reform and stirring and my group in the college embraced all this and became somewhat notorious.

HB: How many of you were there in this "Lutheran Circle", as it were?

MJ: There were about a dozen of us, out of a class of only 160.

HB: Did many of the others also go on to graduate school and other such activities?

MJ: Yes, they all went on to some kind of higher education. One got a master's in social work, one became a lawyer, but no one else became a scholar. I'm the only one who took that particular path.

When I left I was quite alienated. The faculty had refused to put me forward for any of the national fellowships that you could compete for, like the Woodrow Wilson Fellowship, because of my attitude.

I still remember the day that the head nun called me in to tell me. She had been very good to me, and she was practically weeping, she was so upset. It took me a long time—as in 48 years—to forgive them for that, because you just don't do that to a kid, even if the kid's a pain in the ass.

The fact was that I was an A student and I was going off to do graduate work at Cornell. What more did they want?

HB: But you did forgive them eventually. What tipped the balance after 48 years? That's a long time.

MJ: Well, my closest friend in those years is still my closest friend today, and she kept me in touch with all of the other classmates in our circle. When the 50th reunion came along she had been put in charge of it, and I just felt that I had to go.

I was flying to Amsterdam that evening, so I could only stay until 3 pm or so, and as I was just about to leave I went over to one of the quite elderly nuns, who must have been about 95 or so. I leaned over to her and said, "*Sister, it's Peg Candee.*"

She stood straight upright and turned to me and said, "*Ah! You've become a famous scholar!*"

And I just burst into tears. I was just so overwhelmed that she had noticed that I had gone off and done these things, that she valued what I had done, and that, given another life or a different era, she might very well have done the same (in fact, she was a very fine teacher of English literature). It was just this incredible moment for me: it felt that the slate was suddenly wiped clean. And then I went off to Amsterdam.

Questions for Discussion:

1. Do you think it's easier or harder for historians to "do the history of their own people"?

2. Is rebelliousness an important character attribute to have in order to become a great scholar?

II. Decrypting Newton

From physics to theology

HB: But while you advanced into historical scholarship, it seems to me that you were always indulging aspects of your scientific interests and passions. You were looking at the effect and impact of science through the secularization process, the process of societal transformation, and so on.

Is it fair to say that this is a subject that's never really left you, that looking at the impact and the role of science in society is something that you've constantly been engaged with throughout your research career?

MJ: Yes, I think that's right.

If I were to try to boil it down, all along I've been interested in the impact of the Newtonian synthesis on religion, on social formations, on thought in general, on scientific clubs; and even, in this extended way, on Freemasonry, because Freemasons give credence to the "Grand Architect of the Universe" and that sort of thing.

Always in the back of my mind, there's been this interest in what happens in a culture where, suddenly, for the first time ever, you have a law that actually explains the way the planets move and it will enable you to predict where a planet will be at any given time. And it works uniformly—in China, in England, wherever.

This captured the imagination of European thinkers in the 18th century: no one was remote from it. It also captured the attention of critics of the established order who could then argue that human beings could construct order without absolute monarchs, or the boot of the church in one's face, or what have you.

I had a very shrewd mentor, Henry Guerlac, who, in the mid-sixties when I was in grad school, was going into the Newton papers, which had almost been totally unexplored up until that point. They only came into the public domain in the late 1930s.

HB: Why did it take so long?

MJ: Well, they were owned privately, and they came up for sale at Sotheby's in 1936, I believe. At that time, institutions were struggling financially and the University of Cambridge sent John Maynard Keynes down to London to decide whether they were worth bidding on. Out of that experience he wrote a wonderful article that is still read today, called "Newton, the Man."

Anyway, what he saw was that there were thousands of pages of alchemy, not to mention theology, and whatnot. And the university, in its unwisdom, decided that they didn't want the alchemy: all they wanted was the math, physics and a little bit of the theology.

So those papers rattled around for a while until, eventually, a Jewish book-dealer in New York named Abraham Yahuda bought all the theology and alchemy papers and took them to New York. After his death, his widow gave them to Hebrew University in Jerusalem, but the physics, mathematics, natural philosophy and some theology was in Cambridge, and that's where Henry Guerlac went and worked on them.

Henry had an eye for religious and philosophical themes and issues; and he saw Newton, in many of his manuscripts, struggling with how to express the relationship between matter and spirit, which is central to the break that science ultimately causes.

He brought back a xerox copy of a draft that Newton had written of the 23rd Query, which became the famous 31st Query. In this draft, Newton says, "*...And all of nature is attended with signs of life.*"

Henry gave it to me and said, "*Tell me what you make of this. What do you think he's doing here?*"

I had done a master's thesis on the English freethinker John Toland, and the issue in that period was Spinozism. And it all just began to fit into place: that Newton was trying to come to terms with the attack that was being launched on his thinking by people who were saying, "*Ah, Newton's science proves that motion is inherent in matter and that spirit and matter are one in the same,*" which is Spinozism, or Pantheism. That sort of got me going; and my first book (*The Radical Enlightenment*) came out of that.

HB: Right. So, a small digression. The notion of the "Radical Enlightenment" was a phrase that was coined by you, I believe, and has subsequently been embellished upon—primarily but not exclusively—by Jonathan Israel.

And my sense is that you believe there is a little bit too much of an emphasis on Spinoza in his interpretation of this notion of "Radical Enlightenment". Is that a fair comment?

MJ: Absolutely. Spinoza is important; so too is Hobbes; so too is a vast body of clandestine literature, the origins of which we'll never know. But the world does not begin and end with Spinoza.

We could digress further about my differences with Jonathan, but that doesn't seem to me to be very important.

Questions for Discussion:

1. Do you think that Newton's work on alchemy and theology are just as historically significant as his work on physics and mathematics? Would you characterize the University of Cambridge's decision to focus on Newton's writings on math and physics as a form of "historical censorship" or "prudent editing"?

2. What do you think Margaret means, exactly, when she refers to "the break that science ultimately causes"?

III. Beyond the Numbers
Searching for causes

HB: Let's move now to *The First Knowledge Economy: Human Capital and the European Economy, 1750-1850*. I realize that there's a huge gap between that work and what we've just been talking about, but my understanding is that this is, in a way, the third of a trilogy of books that you've now written, together with *The Cultural Meaning of the Scientific Revolution* and *Scientific Culture and the Making of the Industrial West*. Was it designed that way somehow?

MJ: No, it was never actually meant to be the third of a trilogy, it just sort of happened that way. I put forward this thesis in *The Cultural Meaning of the Scientific Revolution* that there was a link between the new science from Descartes, Boyle and Newton to industrial development and that this linkage had not been previously understood. I then complimented that with a series of case studies and published those in 1997. This new book is a return, again, to the topic and an embrace of even more case studies because I had funding to once again go to The Low Countries, as well as France and England.

HB: You still call it "The Low Countries"? You do realize that that's about 300 years out of date, right?

MJ: I know, I know. It's a very early-modern phrase, I must confess. At any rate, I also did more case studies in England. And no matter where I went, it seemed to me that the archival material leapt out and said, *"These industrial entrepreneurs are on the factory floor trying to apply scientific principles, and they leave us a very fulsome record of them doing just that."*

There was a 32-page review of it by Cormac Ó Gráda, who claims that none of that is true and that the key to the Industrial Revolution is the advent of semi-literate tinkerers. That thesis has been repeated over and over; so I figure that, after three tries at it now, if they don't get it, they never will.

HB: I'd like to move to the responses to your work shortly, but let's first back up all the way to this mixture of your scientific orientation and this field of research. I have a personal question for you.

When I was reading your book, it occurred to me that I didn't know very much about how these machines actually worked. I'm fairly familiar with the basic scientific principles, but in terms of what was actually going on and how they functioned, I didn't know very much at all. And it strikes me that this might be a really fun thing to do, to look at these machines carefully.

And it turns out that if you go to Wikipedia, there are all these wonderful animations and very clear descriptions about how these original machines work—from the Newcomen engine all the way up to the Watt steam engine. I spent a fair amount of time playing around and looking at those.

Is that intellectually interesting for you as well, the idea of actually really getting into the mechanics of this, together with the obvious historical perspective?

MJ: Yes, it is to the extent that I too go on the Internet and look at these moving pieces. I've also gone to various industrial sites in Britain where you can see one of the old engines actually at work.

But what interests me more than the actual putting together of the thing was the people who tried to apply scientific principles to make them work.

The problem of friction, for example, is an absolutely fundamental one, and various approaches were taken, some of them purely manual—I think it's wrong to separate science and manual labour, I think they belong together. I can show John Marshall in his Leeds textile factory trying to apply Newtonian principles to the operation of bobbins and to the problem of friction.

In my opinion, then, it's wrong to see all of this as separated. *We* are the ones, *our* sociology, that creates "The History of Science", "The History of Technology", "The History of Music" and so forth, but that's not the way that human beings actually experience the world.

HB: That seems to be a constant refrain—this idea of fighting back against these somewhat trite, interpretive clichés of what actually happened.

You make the point several times throughout *The First Knowledge Economy* that there are these economic historians who say that the reason why the Industrial Revolution happened in the UK from 1750 to 1850 is because wages were very high, there was lots of coal, and things just naturally progressed from these two factors. Of course, there are other theories too: you just mentioned this hypothesis of a bunch of people tinkering around on the factory floor.

For me, as somebody who hasn't thought very much about this, I didn't really ask myself why the Industrial Revolution happened in the UK as opposed to somewhere else. I guess my attitude was that it basically had to have happened somewhere at some point, so it was all pretty arbitrary.

However, when I was reading your book, I started thinking that perhaps that wasn't actually true: it didn't *necessarily* have to have happened at any one particular place. In fact, you can unwind that argument all the way back and say that one can imagine, in a possible world where people were just tinkering, it might have happened in Ancient Rome or some other places thousands of years before.

And that gets you starting to think about what the precursors necessarily were, which brings you into this Newtonian world view and the systematic, law-like nature of things, this notion of applying technology and so forth.

But let me back up a bit and ask something a bit more focused: help give me a sense of context of your field. Is this rigid, economic, historical view that you're emphatically and convincingly railing against throughout your book, is that still the prevailing view among many historians of the period?

MJ: I think the statue has cracked now, and there are economic historians who are increasingly concerned with culture, trying to figure out how you fit cultural explanations into this phenomenon of industrial development. What still prevails, I would say, among the majority of practitioners of economic history, is a desire to find *the* single, sufficient cause.

HB: The silver bullet, as it were.

MJ: Right. Whether it's abundant coal, high wages, semi-literate tinkerers, there's a sense that, *There's got to be* **one thing** *that really causes this*; and I think that's a very flawed way of doing history.

Now, people may turn around and say, "*Well, you're saying that science is* **the one key**." But what I'm really saying is that it's just *one* key. You can't understand what happens on the ground unless you look at these people as thinking entrepreneurs and capitalists who are trying to work out problems. They're bringing to bear the knowledge that they've learned in school, in private study groups, in scientific societies, and all kinds of places. If you leave that out of the story, you impoverish it.

HB: OK, so, that makes a lot of sense—this notion that things are more complex than we might sometimes try to make them in retrospect—that there are a lot of different factors that were at play.

And in your book you ask what I think are the obvious follow-up questions, which are, "*Okay, let's test this thesis by looking at what happens elsewhere. What happens in France? What happens in Belgium? What happens in the Netherlands?*"

And you conclude that this recipe of the combination of high wages and all this coal lying around inevitably leading to the Industrial Revolution doesn't actually hold water. There are exceptions all over the place. Of course, obviously you have to have some access to coal, otherwise you're not going to be able to move forwards; and equally obviously you need some clear economic incentive to mechanize as well. But at the risk of being simplistic myself, I must admit that the whole situation is a bit confusing to me.

If you have a thesis and it doesn't really hold up very well by looking at the obvious points of comparison (France, The Low Countries, Scotland, wherever), then it strikes me as a good time to change your thesis. So, I guess my question—finally— is: *Do other people do the same sort of analysis you do and somehow come to different conclusions so that they're able to maintain their original thesis, maintain that they were right all along? Or do they not even bother looking in the first place?*

MJ: Generally speaking, with the exception of someone like Joel Mokyr, most economic historians look for, first of all, what can be quantified in a particular site. They look for figures on wages, for example, or coal extraction, or whatever.

But very few actually go on the ground and look to see what's being taught in the educational system, what's in the textbooks, what's taken out of the textbooks at certain periods and put back in the textbooks later, and so forth.

That kind of work is very qualitative: you actually have to go into archives and sit and read a great deal to find out what's going on. That's not the kind of research that economic historians are taught. That's not their métier.

Which is fine, but there are different ways of doing history; and the way I'm doing it, I think—I hope—is closer to the way human beings experience the world.

HB: Okay, so you're the historian and I'm not; but it seems to me that there's a role for people to do the sort of quantitative analysis you were referring to earlier: to collect that data, to examine the numbers in detail and so forth.

It should be explicitly mentioned that you do some of this in your work as well, and I'm sure there's more still that could be done: comparing wages, looking at purchasing power and rates of exchange, economic incentives, return on investment and all the rest of that. And all of that is clearly very important.

But that seems to me to be a different sort of activity than coming up with a grand thesis explaining why the Industrial Revolution happened at this time and why it happened over here as opposed to over there. There seems to be a huge disconnect for me.

In other words, it seems to me that if you're going to focus on these quantitative arguments and dig down deep into the economic data, then that's certainly an important thing to be doing, but it's not necessarily going to lead to some grand, synthetic thesis on why something as significant and as major as the Industrial Revolution could have possibly happened at this time and place as opposed to another.

MJ: Well, if you were to say to someone like Bob Allen, "*Okay, let's say you're right, that the wages were highest in Britain*"—in fact, that's not really true, they were very high in the Dutch Republic, if not higher than Britain, but whatever—"*These people living and breathing in Britain in the 1770s and 1780s, **they** don't know that their wages are higher than anywhere else in the world.*"

HB: Right. It's not like they can take a particular factory and outsource it or something.

MJ: That's right; they don't know anything about this. They're working on the ground with what they've got; and one of the basic principles of economic life is that you always try to minimize your costs wherever you can and increase your profits. This is not rocket science.

So to say that the high wages in Britain are both distinctive and the motivating factor turns out to be problematic, because they're actually *not* that distinctive; and this argument of the motivating factor relies upon a more fundamental assumption—which often goes unstated in the economic history literature—and that is that people are "driven by the numbers": they understand immediately that something is "too expensive" and so they go about finding ways to make it less expensive.

Well, there's not a lot of evidence for this. If you look at the figures of what's being paid to coal miners in 18th-century Newcastle, nothing's changing: wages were very low and remained low throughout the century. So the whole notion that it's the high cost of wages...

In fact, what you discover when you really go into a mine, look at the wage structure, and see what the engineers say about their expenses, is that the single biggest expense that they keep recording is the cost of horses: *feeding* the horses. Now, the cost of feeding a horse in France versus the cost of feeding a horse in Britain cannot be that different.

These guys are *not* telling you that what's killing them and their factory is the cost of wages. They're not saying, *"I've got to do everything I can to reduce the labour force, so I'm going to mechanize."* They're not saying that.

In order to advance that argument, you have to begin with an assumption that certain things move human beings more than others, that they have an instinctive feel for a high-wage setting and will do whatever they have to do to undo that.

And that is an assumption about the way human beings work that I don't think life experience bears out.

Questions for Discussion:

1. To what extent can we ever be certain that we understood why certain historical events happened the way that they did?

2. How do you think an "economic historian" might respond to Margaret's objections outlined in this chapter?

IV. Apprenticeship
Pivotal time to develop

HB: I'd like to discuss education. You talk a lot about formal education systems in your book, comparing and contrasting them in different countries, how it was being affected by the other things that were going on—wars, revolutions and so forth—but you also talk about societies that were founded, the education that was conveyed *informally*, either by travellers passing through from other lands, societies and so on.

And another thing that struck me that I hadn't really appreciated was the role of the apprentice. It seems that this was a fairly standard practice—didn't James Watt go off to become a carpenter or something when he was younger?

MJ: A clockmaker. He was an apprentice to a clockmaker.

HB: Right. So there was this notion of, as it were, "getting one's hands dirty", because you can talk about being imbued with the Newtonian synthesis and the law-like nature of reality and the fact that you can predict comets and tides and so forth, but I'm guessing that unless you're actually out there doing stuff, it's all pretty abstract.

And that seems to be a significant part of the ethos of the time that the British were really focusing on. Perhaps it wasn't a deliberate policy as such, but it certainly was a route that people were taking that wound up having an enormous influence.

MJ: I think it's incontrovertible that the British apprenticeship system was possibly the best in Europe but it's also the case that the Dutch apprentice system was also very important, active and enforcing;

and it was further reinforced by the power of the guilds because they remained very strong in the Dutch Republic.

HB: Right, which is presumably why the salaries were so high there, as you were saying earlier.

MJ: Yes. But I don't want to diminish at all the importance of the apprentice experience. The example I would use would be James Watt himself. Watt is apprentice to a clockmaker, and he begins life cutting out numbers for the faces of clocks.

At night, he has a tutor who's tutoring him in 's Gravesande, the basic Newtonian textbooks of the period. When he finishes his apprenticeship, he goes out and presents himself to the world as an engineer. He knows trigonometry, he knows Newtonian science; but did he get all that from his apprenticeship? No, he did not. What the apprenticeship did give him was that seven-year time period in which he could learn all of these other things.

HB: Again, it's this combination of factors. And this more general education, it seems, was valued sociologically, to the extent that it was broadly encouraged and "in the air", perhaps.

MJ: Yes. If you were a man of business and there was a little bit of surplus money in the household you would send your sons out to be apprenticed. It was just a smart thing to do. And I think that was universally recognized as something to do for a young man in order to give him a future.

In the opening of the book, I say, "*Many of the people you're going to meet in this book were apprentices. We often don't know with whom or when, because that information hasn't survived. But it's a fair assumption that most of these people were apprenticed at some point.*"

Question for Discussion:

1. How important is it to provide willing students sufficient time to "learn other things"? Might there be lessons in Margaret's anecdote of James Watt learning Newtonian science in the evenings that could be applied to our current educational systems?

V. Religion and Geography
Unitarianism and other factors

HB: You also highlight relevant cultural aspects associated with religion, particularly Unitarianism: that it was accepted, indeed encouraged, to work hard, be productive and make money, while at the same time being a well-respected, moral Christian.

When one considers the impact that such attitudes had in cities like Birmingham and Manchester, it makes me wonder how unique it was compared to what was happening in other Protestant centres?

MJ: Well, Unitarianism is a uniquely Anglo-American phenomenon. I don't think you find Unitarianism in German Protestant lands, and I know you don't find it in the Dutch Republic. You may now, of course, but I'm referring specifically to the 18th century.

It is rather distinctively British, but it very quickly becomes American when it comes over to the New World. By the 1750s there are Unitarian chapels up and down the colonies. It's a religion that has not yet received the kind of historical treatment that it needs.

In the literature, it is always treated as "rational dissent," whatever that means—as if everybody else is irrational. Many historians have repeated the old line of Erasmus Darwin, that *"Unitarianism provided a feather-bed to catch a falling Christian."* This is all wrong—the whole thing is wrong. If I were to do another book, I would do it on Unitarianism.

HB: What would you do, exactly?

MJ: Well, I would go to England and go through the records. There are huge numbers of Unitarian archives just sitting there, and I would go and read the sermons, prayer books, letters and diaries and try to get closer to this mentality of the Unitarian. I have written a little bit about it in a review article on a book about Joseph Priestley and English Unitarianism in America.

HB: My understanding of the importance of Unitarianism to the development of the Industrial Revolution is that it played a major contributing factor in creating a unique social and cultural milieu that enabled people like Matthew Boulton and James Watt to feel that, "*Yes , you can be a good Christian and a good member of society and, at the same time, be making money, be moving forwards with worldly things, be working hard*,"—what we would now call the "Protestant work ethic".

MJ: Well, more than Protestant, it was Calvinist. You get Mennonites, who are a form of "inner-light" people who are an alternative to the strict Calvinism. One of the things that happens in the early 18th century in Protestant Europe—and it's happening quite generally for different reasons in different places—is that there's a growing reluctance to embrace what's called "specific predestination".

General predestination involves an awareness that predestination exists in principle simply because God is the way He is—that is, omniscient—but to apply it to oneself ("specific predestination") seems almost beside the point. So, there's a growing repudiation of this personal view of, "*I'm in this struggle with God.*"

Now, it's not like that completely disappears. There's a wonderful book by Matthew Kadane, a former student of mine, called *The Watchful Clothier*. The book is based upon a 46-volume, personal, spiritual diary of a mid-18th century Leeds clothing maker. His entire life is centered around the struggle with the question of whether, as he grows more and more prosperous, he is risking his own salvation.

Now, he *is* a believer in specific predestination. But there were a lot of people around him, including those who, towards the end of his life in the 1760s, he hears coming to the chapels preaching essentially Unitarian doctrine.

They are saying, *"The notion of the Trinity is irrational; and it's further irrational because it makes Christ be further from us, not closer to us."*

This is what, I think, is very much going on in the Unitarian Movement: it increases Protestant fervour by making Christ into a human being, and thereby renders predestination completely irrelevant.

HB: Another thing you mentioned was that, for the longest time, if you weren't officially Anglican, you couldn't actually go to Oxford or Cambridge.

For me at least, this conjured up images of the ritualistic, Latin-strewn world of Oxford and Cambridge as opposed to the rather earthier environment of these Unitarian-driven dissenters in cities like Birmingham and Manchester and Leeds and Newcastle.

Is it fair to say that this, too, is a contributing factor why the Industrial Revolution happened in the North of England as opposed to in the South?

That, notwithstanding the fact that Newton himself, of course, was in Cambridge, the real application of these ideas naturally involved a different perspective, a different community, a different milieu for such rapid technological change to occur?

MJ: Well, again, if I were to explain why the North versus the South, I would bring in a lot of different factors.

The Southern counties, the "home counties" are agriculturally among the richest in the world. To this day, they produce a yield that is incredible. So, big farming dominates the South in a way that it doesn't in the North—there's not much you can grow around Newcastle. So, that's one piece of the story.

The other piece is that the Northern towns, like Birmingham, are unincorporated: that is, they do not have a charter from the Crown; and, basically, they can be run by whomever is important in the community.

So there isn't an Anglican establishment in many of those towns. And then coal was certainly very important. It's also the case that there are probably more non-Anglicans—i.e. dissenters—in these

Northern, unincorporated towns than what you would find in, say, London.

London doesn't have an Industrial Revolution; it's a totally different animal, a commercial and governmental center. Neither does Bristol or Norwich, which are the other big cities in this period.

The economy of Norwich is dominated by the agricultural land surrounding it, while Bristol is dominated by the Atlantic trade.

As time goes on, then, by, say 1820, the industrial development that has occurred in Northern towns is so significant that it just leaves the South behind. When you look for the turning points in the mid-18th century, there are a lot of factors. Dissent is one of them, but also the nature of agriculture and the land, the nature of the government in these towns, access to rivers and so forth.

Questions for Discussion:

1. What do you think the phrase, "Unitarianism provided a feather-bed to catch a falling Christian" means, exactly?

2. To what extent do you think distancing oneself from the notion of "specific predestination" facilitates the accumulation of business success?

3. Do you think the physical separation of Northern England from the main commercial and governmental centre of London played a role in facilitating a culture of independence and innovation?

VI. Theory vs. Practice

France's surprising underdevelopment

HB: I'd like to keep playing the counterfactual game a little bit more, if you don't mind. You mentioned how France was relatively slow to industrialize, which in some ways is quite surprising given their role as such a key player—arguably ***the*** key player—in the Enlightenment.

You point out the potential impact of their rapidly changing educational system as a relevant factor, due to the turbulence of the Revolution and Napoleon's presence. As I understand it, for a time, during the Revolution and beyond, there was a significant focus on adapting the education system, putting far more emphasis on science and scientific ways of thinking.

Then, after Napoleon falls from power and the monarchy is restored in 1815, there is the impact of the Catholic church when everything becomes once again rigidified and all of these reforms basically get thrown out the window until at least 1830 and the next revolution.

So, finally, my counterfactual question is: *If this didn't happen, do you think that France would have been able to catch up much faster, or were there additional factors that were also at play?*

MJ: Well, I'm sure there were other factors. The only counterfactual that would prove the argument to be that France would have caught up is Belgium.

The Belgian educational system accepts the reforms of the French Revolution and then it gets repudiated. There's a struggle about the secular nature of the system all throughout the 19th century but they don't actually take science out of the curriculum.

What shocked me—and I've been in a lot of archives—was when I went to Northern France to closely examine what was being taught in the schools there from about 1815 onwards, I saw that, in school after school, there was no science or math. They just took it out of the curriculum, or it fell away because nobody cared.

I don't know why this happened, but it happened. And it's consonant with the prevailing ideology, which was that science was one of the causes of the French Revolution. Had that not happened, had the French continued with educational reforms that enhanced scientific education and introduced more and more machinery into the actual classrooms and schools, I think they probably would have had a better go at it than they had. But as it was, they were significantly retarded by 1850.

HB: I guess the thing that I find confusing is that the French have had such an exemplary record in terms of pure mathematics over the last few hundred years—even to this day. The French have a very strong tradition in pure math.

So, I certainly appreciate the idea of the Catholic Church reasserting their control over the educational program in the wake of the Revolution, but I wonder if there isn't something else going on in terms of pure versus applied, abstract versus concrete and applied.

As I was saying before, they really are very different: just because you happen to be gifted in advanced mathematics doesn't mean that you necessarily have an orientation or desire to start applying these concepts to the real world.

On the one hand, there are cultural, economic and societal motivations as you were describing, but there are also intellectual traditions. I can imagine a society which is incredibly mathematically literate, but doesn't actually do much in terms of developing applications, and I'm wondering if that might be related to what we're talking about in 19th-century France. What are your thoughts on that?

MJ: Well, it's true that the purity of mathematics and the purity of philosophy and all of those abstract skills are, in France, even to this day, associated with the highly intelligent élites who can be gleaned out of the school system and placed in their top academic institutions, their *grandes écoles*.

That system is a throwback to an *ancien régime* culture. Is that a factor in France's relative disinterest in industry? It may be.

Questions for Discussion:

1. How useful do you think counterfactual questions are to sharpening one's understanding of historical processes?

2. What role do you think anti-British sentiment might have played in France's relatively late embrace of the Industrial Revolution?

VII. Lessons Learned?

Towards cultivating the innovative spirit

HB: I cut you off earlier when you were talking about responses. You've written three of these books now; and my sense is that a constant theme throughout is your insistence that we have to go beyond these often simplistic theses that have limited our understanding in the past, we have to integrate a broad, socio-cultural, political background, education, economics, and many more factors besides. Is that view gaining any ground, by and large?

MJ: I think so, to the extent that I'm hearing about conferences devoted to the question of economics and culture. There's a growing sense among graduate students in economic history that the old models leave something to be desired. I don't follow the developments of economic history that closely, but my sense is that there is a sea-change going on.

HB: Often authors don't independently or exclusively independently choose their own titles, so I thought I'd ask: *The First Knowledge Economy*—whose idea was it to call it that?

MJ: That's a good question. It might very well have come from my Cambridge editor. I'd have to go back into my computer and see what I was calling those chapters early on.

HB: Right, but are you happy with the title?

MJ: Oh, yes. It's fine.

HB: Okay, that's good enough. So, my next question is, as you can probably guess: what are the implications of all of this?

I realize that you're a historian and that you neither prognosticate nor engage in public policy as part of your day job, but it seems to me that there are obvious present-day implications of what you're saying.

In particular, this idea of establishing the right cultural milieu in order to make progress, broadly defined: "education", "innovation", "human capital"—these are words that you'll see sprinkled liberally throughout any newspaper today.

Is there something that we might be able to apply from our understanding of what happened in England between 1750 and 1850 to our present day?

MJ: Well, I think this rethinking of what's needed today is already going on, in the sense that the UN, every three or four years, surveys all of the nations that are now considered to be in need of development—I believe there are currently 120—and one of the very first questions that the survey asks is, *What is being taught in science and technology from early on right through to universities?* And those booklets that the UN produces are available.

Similarly, we're hearing this in public-policy debates all the time: the need for better education in science and math.

HB: OK, but, it's easy to say words like "STEM" or "We need more of this," because often what people are really saying is that we need more Googles or better phones. After all, by and large the innovations that are driving economic productivity are scientific and technological ones.

However, that's a very different question than how we should teach it, how it should be culturally appreciated, how we should move forwards as a society, not only in terms of education but also getting back to this notion of this Unitarian ethos you were speaking about earlier.

Because, as I understand it, these guys—as part of their belief in harnessing the laws of nature and being able to apply it—were also trying to do something for their fellow man as they were hard at work developing technological tools and spurning ostentatious displays of wealth. So, I'm thinking somewhat more broadly than just, *"We should have more engineering schools."*

MJ: I think that you're whistling in the graveyard, if you're going to get white Americans to eschew cultures of luxury and ostentation and consumption. It's a lost cause. Forget it. I think where you're going to see this kind of entrepreneurial spirit, the discipline and desire to do good, is among minority groups.

At UCLA, the plurality of our students are Asian-American. I mean, you can engage in all kinds of facile generalizations, but the reality is that, on the whole, they work harder. They just do. Of course there are exceptions, but they bring with them a different culture from what is in the mainstream of American culture now, and I don't think that this is going to change much.

I think it has to come from foreigners who are coming with their own agendas and own culture. They will assimilate into American society I am sure, but in the process they will change it.

HB: OK. But on the other hand, there's a very strong, philanthropic tradition in this country; it's very unique and it still exists.

If you talk to captains of industry, they'll tell you that their job is to make as much money as possible and then reinvest it for future generations—and that's also part of this legacy, I suspect. Well, maybe not. At any rate, whether or not it can be traced back that way is immaterial: it certainly exists in this culture. It's part of the fabric of this society.

There are many philanthropic foundations throughout this country. I'm just wondering if there might be an opportunity to play on that a little bit more, explicitly recognizing what has gone on before, and tying that to more of a secular, naturalistic agenda.

MJ: I could very well imagine a foundation that wants to put money into trying to develop curricula that look more like what you're talking about. I mean, one of the things that we've done right in America as opposed to Europe—and I mean all of Western Europe—is that we give tax write-offs for charity.

That doesn't happen in France, the Netherlands, Britain and so forth. Here, if you give—depending on your tax bracket, say, 20,000 dollars—the government winds up giving nine of it. That is an enormous advantage, and we desperately have to ensure that we keep that, because these kinds of innovations, I agree, are going to come from private sources: foundations and entrepreneurs. It's not going to come out of your mainstream, educational infrastructure, which is basically trying just to cope.

Questions for Discussion:

1. Do you agree with Margaret that the future of America's entrepreneurial spirit lies with its immigrants?

2. What role can government have in promoting widespread technological and cultural change?

VIII. History Today
Reflections on research and teaching

HB: We compared various countries during this time period—Britain, France, Belgium, the Netherlands, and so on. But as people are now looking more and more at global history, there's the broader question of *Why did this phenomenon happen in **Europe**, as opposed to elsewhere in the world?*

Does the act of asking these sorts of broader global historical questions interest you at all?

MJ: It does and it doesn't. The thing that troubles me about these kinds of global questions like, "*Why Europe? Why not China in the 17th century?*" is that the people who ask these questions, by and large, do not read Chinese or Japanese or whatever. They don't really know those cultures.

So, the answers that they're putting together would ring about as true to somebody in those cultures who really knows them as it does when I read somebody writing about the Dutch Republic in the early modern period who doesn't know Dutch. I mean, what are we talking about here? We're taking everything from secondary sources and trying to tell a story about a place that we really don't know; and that seems to me to characterize a great deal of what goes on in the so-called "global approach".

HB: How, more broadly, is the field of history changing? We just touched on the notion of "global history"? Are there other changes that are interesting to you? Depressing to you?

MJ: Well, I think one change that's very interesting is that national histories qua national histories are falling gradually into disfavour. I'm seeing job ads all the time for people in British history who "do the Atlantic world", or people in French history who can "do francophone Africa" and so on and so forth.

Dutch history has benefited enormously from this because, of course, it's among the very first global empires, so Dutch history is, in this milieu, flourishing. How far we can go in escaping the national histories is unclear.

Certainly, American history is alive and well and thriving, and I don't see us finding a way to generalize too much. Ideally one would like to do North American history to include Canada and the United States, but it's not happening.

Do I see depressing trends? There's too much adjunct labour, there's too much farming out, but the financials of the American academy are very much a result of larger economic forces and the attitudes of the electorate.

HB: Is there enough of a societal appreciation of the importance of historical research?

MJ: That's very hard for me to say. Certainly, I have been treated extremely well by the American academy and my work has been appreciated. Are there efforts being made to downplay the humanities? Some people say that this is happening all over the country.

HB: But I'm talking to you. What do you think?

MJ: I don't see it. I don't see it in my own world. I don't see anyone for a second suggesting that what we're doing in the social sciences or the humanities is inferior to what's being done in the so-called "hard sciences".

HB: Do you see any evidence of lowering of academic standards or "dumbing down"?

MJ: Dumbing down? Again, it depends upon the circumstances, it depends upon the kind of students that you get. Are we giving more A's now than we were 50 years ago? Well, I've been teaching now almost 50 years. I'm not giving more, but maybe somebody else is.

I don't know. It depends a lot on the writing skills. For us, writing is absolutely critical; and one thing that has changed in the last twenty years is that writing has improved. The high schools are doing a much better job.

HB: Well, that's good. I don't hear that very often.

MJ: I know, but this is what I'm seeing.

HB: What about the field of historical scholarship, in terms of how one goes about one's day job as a professional historian? How is that changing, in your view? When I talked to John Elliott (*The Passionate Historian*) some time ago, he spoke about how modern technology is both helping and, to some extent, hindering the historical process.

He mentioned how one can now be sitting at home, looking at documents where computer imagery could remove ink stains from the original, thereby enabling you to read documents that you might not have been able to before, as well as the ease of being able to sit at home and have access to a tremendous variety of documented material—which would normally require an enormous amount of time and travel and effort—and how that was a wonderful thing for a historian.

But at the same time, he spoke of the fact that these very developments reduce the opportunities for people to go into a culture, into a society and into the world of archives and immerse oneself physically, as well as mentally in the culture; and he speculated that this might have some deleterious effects.

He wasn't whining or complaining about it, but just commenting that, in all likelihood, that's bound to have some impact on the business of historical research. Do you see it that way as well or do you see it differently?

MJ: I think John's partly right in that the days are gone, I think, where American-based historians researching any non-American topic would be naturally required to live abroad for prolonged periods of time. For me, all told I've lived six or seven years in Europe.

Now, you can vastly reduce the amount of time you have to spend abroad, but I don't know anybody yet—any students I've taught or on whose committees I sit—who has just stopped going to those archives entirely. They just don't go for as long, but I think you still gain a kind of immersion that has to happen, because you still have to go. It may be that in 20 or 30 years from now, we'll be in a world where everything is online, and that will be a different sort of thing. But right now, you still have to go.

Questions for Discussion:

1. Do you feel that a proper sense of respect for history and historical scholarship is being conveyed through the educational system? Is it better or worse than it used to be?

2. Are you surprised by Margaret's comments that student writing skills have increased over the past twenty years?

IX. Past and Future
New books and bizarre faucets

HB: Were you serious about the book project on Unitarianism that you mentioned earlier? And if so, are you just thinking about writing it, or have you actually begun?

MJ: No, right now I'm writing a general book on the Enlightenment that I'm currently calling *The Secular Enlightenment*, but it may be called something else by the time it's finished. I've basically finished the first two chapters: on the secularization of time and the secularization of space.

This sets things in a new framework: space, for example, in terms of both the discovery of the New World and the discovery of the Heavens, which are essentially 16th- and 17th-century phenomena that have an enormous impact in transforming the way that Westerners can think about the world. The next chapter is going to be on the secularization of religion, and I am going to do a section in there on Unitarianism, and I may go and do some archival work.

HB: So, by secularization of religion, you mean the abstracting away of some of the moral components of living a good life from the religious doctrine? What do you mean, exactly?

MJ: No, I mean more in the first instance of the removal of the importance of ritual, ceremony, costumes, the internalization of religion: that it becomes more of a personal thing instead of a sociological structure.

The privatization of religion means that it becomes a place that has its own sphere, and that really is an enormous change in

European history. I think the Unitarians are an extreme example of that, and I will talk a fair bit about them.

I will also talk about Liberal Protestantism, and I'd like to talk about efforts made in Catholic Europe to try to reconcile the Church with the Enlightenment. They don't succeed, by and large, but there are people trying to do that.

I'll talk a little bit about Freemasonry as well, because it just fits into that whole phenomenon of having entirely secular rituals to the "Grand Architect". Now, where I go from there, I'm not sure. I haven't figured out the other four or five chapters yet—these things just kind of turn up in your head.

HB: I have one last question that I'm pretty sure you won't know the answer to, but maybe you will. At any rate, it's bothered me for a very long time.

Almost every time I go to Britain and I find myself in a washroom there are two taps for the hot and cold water, with two separate spouts.

Practically this means that one either burns one's hands or freezes one's hands. Now, this is the place where the Industrial Revolution began, and somehow, they haven't figured out yet that they have to have the one spout and mix the water in the spout before it comes out so that it's temperate for your hands. Why is that, you think?

MJ: Well, we could add to this a discussion of French plumbing, if you'd like.

HB: But my point is that this was the heartland of the Industrial Revolution as it were: they were the ones who were the cock of the walk with the steam engines and coal and trains and all of that—this is where all this tremendously impressive harnessing of science and technology *began*.

But this simply makes no sense to me, and not only can I not see one possible advantage to doing things this way, it should also be pointed out that nowhere else in the modern world are you faced with this nonsense. So it is perplexing to me: what's going on here? Is this a sort of bizarre vestige of historical arcana that refuses to go away? You must have some insight.

MJ: Well, I think what's happening here is that the factories that are producing these things are still doing well and making money.

HB: But how? How is that possible?

MJ: They don't have any foreign competition.

HB: Sure. Because nobody else in the world wants this crazy stuff.

MJ: Right. I mean, there's probably an import tax on foreign equipment.

HB: Well, I know I'm getting way outside your comfort zone, but this has been driving me crazy for years, and I thought that a historian of the Industrial Revolution might be able to shed some light on it.

MJ: Well, we put in a new bathroom downstairs 15 years ago. I don't remember why, but we wound up buying hardware that was made outside of Manchester from a British company, and this was the worst stuff I'd ever seen. You want to talk shoddy? This gave a whole new meaning to shoddy. And it was being sold in this luxury shop in Beverly Hills and we had this contract with them, so we got the products at half price and all that.

It's an old saw that industrializing late can be as beneficial as industrializing early: you put these factories and infrastructure into place and then you don't change anything, for decades sometimes, or centuries.

I mean, in the late 19th century, there were steam engines working in factories all over Britain that had been put in 50 or 60 years earlier.

They were not state-of-the-art by any means, shape or form, but the people who had these factories with these engines were making a nice profit—they didn't want to expand and become global, they were quite content staying the way they were.

Many of these are family businesses, and I'll bet this company whose products I bought is a family business as well that's not on the open stock market. They've probably been feeding generations quite comfortably off this equipment that once was probably state-of-the-art but now is a piece of junk. So, that's the best answer that I can give you.

Questions for Discussion:

1. If you had the time and expertise to write a work of history, what would it be about?

2. Can you give other examples of early technological innovators who rested on their laurels and eventually became eclipsed by their competitors? Is there any way to avoid becoming a "victim of one's success" in this way?

X. Righting Wrongs, Slowly

Gender discrimination in the academy

HB: Anything else you'd like to add? Anything I've missed?

MJ: Well, we have not talked about women in the historical profession. I don't know whether I'm the person to do that, but someone needs to.

HB: Well, you're right here. Go for it.

MJ: OK, here I am.

Well, this has been a struggle of monumental proportions. I mean, don't for a second imagine, when you talk to a woman of my age in the profession, that she has had an easy time of it because of gender.

I just went to London to commemorate the life of Helli Koenigsberger—who was great friends with John Elliott, by the way. Helli was my teacher; and one of the first things that I said at the round table was, *"The great thing about Helli was that he didn't hit on you. He left you alone. Men and women were all the same to him. He did not think that he had some sort of seignorial rights."*

HB: And the very fact that that's worth commenting on means that his was a relatively unique case.

MJ: Exactly. There was so much of that going on. I mean, I was a teaching assistant to a lovely man—Pearce Williams, a historian of science—who openly said, and he didn't care who heard him and was not being mean, *"There will never be a woman hired in this department: over my dead body."*

When I started in the '60s, there was not *one* major research university in this country that had a tenured woman in the history department.

HB: And you were telling me before that in 1977...

MJ: That I was the first woman to be appointed a fellow at the School of History Studies at the Institute for Advanced Study.

Somebody's got to write this all up so that we all remember what this was like. I led the floor fight at The American Historical Association in the early 1970s, where the resolution on the floor was that every department in the country that was a member of The American Historical Association had to publicly advertise jobs.

And Jack Hexter got up—he was an officer of the Association—and he fought this tooth and nail.

Then I got up and said, *"Jack, you've spoken for the court, now let me get up and speak for the country."*

These people were ruthless in defending their privileges and their right to appoint their male students to whatever job they got their hands on. That was part of the culture into the 1990s, and only now are we finally getting gender-balanced, though there really still isn't a major department in the country that is 50/50 or even 40/60.

HB: But if you're a woman today who's just completed her PhD in history at UCLA, say, and now going on the job market, are you likely to face discrimination?

MJ: No. Now you're likely to be privileged over your male counterpart because every department in the country is under a mandate for more gender balance. So, my female students do better, by and large.

Meanwhile one of my colleague Lynn Hunt's very best students, spent three years going from postdoc to postdoc before finally getting a job at the University of Toronto.

HB: I know that in the natural sciences it's customary to do many postdocs. That's now become quite standard in your field, as well?

MJ: Yes. Every research university offers them now in historical sciences.

HB: Is there now an expectation that, when you get your PhD, you're going to do that?

MJ: No, the expectation is still that you'll go directly into the job market but the postdoc is a fallback.

HB: And on the ground, as it were, within a department, if you're a woman graduate student, if you're a woman faculty member, are there any issues, by and large?
   For the most part, is it fair to say that it's now a convivial, congenial work environment without a great deal of discrimination? I'm not asking about UCLA in particular, I'm just saying, if one can generalize, is it the case that the work environment, in American universities at least, is largely sexist-free?

MJ: I wouldn't say it's sexist-free, but it's night and day compared to what it used to be.

HB: Does it still have any appreciable way to go, or is it basically okay now?

MJ: Well, many departments, mine included, have never had a female chair.

HB: Even now?

MJ: Nope. There's just a way in which that somehow doesn't work out.

HB: Well, often people don't want to be the chair. Maybe it's just a sign of probity on the part of the women.

MJ: Exactly—a sign of sanity. But on the administrative level, it's also still harder for women to climb up to be provost and president and that sort of thing. Remember when Drew Faust became president of Harvard—it was a major event and in the front pages of all the newspapers. And that was only in 2007. So there are plenty of glass ceilings out there, but they're all showing signs of cracks. It's just a very different world.

HB: Anything else?

MJ: Nope, I think we've covered it all.

HB: Well, thanks a lot. That was most enjoyable.

MJ: You're very welcome.

Questions for Discussion:

1. Do you think that discriminating against men for academic faculty jobs is justified in light of past practices?

2. To what extent do you think the prevailing sexist attitudes towards women in academe impacted historical scholarship of the time?

Continuing the Conversation

Readers who enjoyed this discussion are referred to Margaret's books, *The First Knowledge Economy: Human Capital and the European Economy, 1750-1850*, *The Secular Enlightenment*, *The Cultural Meaning of the Scientific Revolution* and *Scientific Culture and the Making of the Industrial West*.

Science and Pseudoscience

A conversation with Michael Gordin

Introduction

Harnessing the Fringe

Years ago, when I found myself in charge of a theoretical physics institute, I used to receive a steady stream of letters and emails from highly frustrated, would-be-scientific revolutionaries, anxious to tell me about their work.

Typically, they would explain how the scientific community had rejected them out of hand on sociological grounds, simply because their work went too far against the prevailing orthodoxy. Often they would compare their circumstances—if not themselves—to those of Einstein, struggling away in secret with his transformative ideas about the universe while working at a Swiss patent office. Inevitably, too, it might bear mentioning, they were all men.

I quickly learned that any physicist who has ever been in any position of authority anywhere has received a significant number of such letters. The most common response is to simply ignore them. My approach was always to write back a short reply thanking them for their time and effort, but explaining that I didn't have the time to go through their work in proper detail. If they had, indeed, found some transformative insight, I responded evenly, I urged them to formally submit their results to the appropriate journals for consideration like everybody else.

Of course, this was somewhat duplicitous. I knew very well that the reason they had approached me (in addition to virtually anyone else they could find an email address for) was that no established journal would ever seriously consider wading through their invariably dense wad of notes, let alone publishing it.

What passed for a certain form of politeness, then, was hardly anything that justified my place on a higher moral plane—like everyone else, I, too, hoped that these fringe figures would just go away and leave me alone.

Yet, in the back of my mind, I always wondered. Not, as it happens, that their claims of possessing a revolutionary insight might turn out to be correct—I am sceptical enough to believe that the chances of that happening were, statistically, vanishingly small—but more sociologically speaking: what keeps these people going, day after day, perpetually encountering an unequivocal wall of rejection, if not outright hostility, from the scientific authorities? Why wilfully remain mired on the "outside" of the big tent of science? After all, the global scientific effort is quite different now than it was more than a century ago in Einstein's day. For anyone anxious to make some sort of a contribution to the scientific effort, there is always somewhere that will accept you to at least do an undergraduate degree, if not a PhD.

The cynical answer is that they are all simply crazy and don't have the intellectual resources necessary to make their way through even the most basic technical material, let alone a doctoral program somewhere. But something about that response always struck me as being too pat. Doubtless it was the case for some. But likely not all.

So it was with a particular interest that I picked up Michael Gordin's intriguing book, *The Pseudoscience Wars: Immanuel Velikovsky and the Birth of the Modern Fringe*. I am old enough to (just barely) remember the name Immanuel Velikovsky, the charismatic rebel who wrote (among others) the bestselling book *Worlds in Collision* that managed to provocatively combine unbridled scientific speculation with ancient myth.

By all accounts, Velikovsky was a decidedly curious character. The notorious Russian-born doctor-turned psychoanalyst-turned astronomer-historian-autodidact not only had a flair for writing and boatloads of charisma and energy, he also was on record for making a couple of concrete predictions of his radical new theory of the solar system that turned out, much to the dismay of the authorities of the day, to actually be correct.

Here, then, was a specific, compelling, historical instance that could be carefully studied to examine how science had deliberately separated itself from pseudoscience, and why.

The full story of Immanuel Velikovsky turns out to be even more fascinating than one might expect, combining elements of Freudian psychoanalysis, Cold War paranoia, ancient mythology, NASA press conferences, 1960s counterculture and a good deal more besides. It's not too hard to see why Michael, as a professional historian of science, would pick such a captivatingly good yarn.

But to me, always lurking in the background were the broader issues: *How do we distinguish science from pseudoscience? How **should** we? Is science too conservative? Too liberal? Can we improve its process? Can we learn from the past?*

So when I got the chance to catch up with Michael face to face, I was anxious to steer the conversation towards those more general questions. Perhaps unsurprisingly, it turned out that he was as well.

One of the first things he wanted to mention was that, in stark contrast to contemporary scientific dogma, Karl Popper's famous falsifiability criterion is hardly the magic bullet to meaningfully distinguish science from pseudoscience.

> *"It's a very appealing criterion. Except it's got a couple of problems. The first problem is, **How do you know that you falsified something?** If it were the case that every time an experiment with a null result meant that you'd falsified something, then everything we know about physics and chemistry will be wrong because high school students around the world have failed to replicate it. So you have to do the experiment **right**. But how do you know you've done the experiment right, unless you get 'the right result'?*
>
> *"The second problem is that any valuable demarcation criterion has to cut the world in the right place: we want to make sure that all*

*the things that we regard as science are scientific, and those things that we think of as 'fringe' or 'pseudo' are not. It should divide that well. The problem is that there are lots of sciences which have a very hard time coming up with falsifying instances—in particular, the historically-engaged sciences like evolutionary theory, geology, cosmology and so forth. You can't rerun the tape. If someone tells you, '**The universe was created this way,**' and you respond, '**Well, but what's the falsifiable statement?**' it's awfully hard to find one.*

*"The third problem with Popper's criterion is a philosophical one: it requires you to not believe in truth. Consistently applying it means that **nothing** is ever true: scientists make no true claims. I can't say, '**This chair is made of atoms**'. I can only say, '**No one has disproved the claim that this chair is made of atoms, yet.**' It's a very uncomfortable position to be in long term."*

Michael believes that there is, in principle, no obvious "bright line of demarcation" that we can use to separate science from pseudo-science. But, contrary to what you might suppose, he hardly finds this disturbing.

In fact, he believes that by consistently exhibiting a willingness to engage (albeit in a limited way) with "the fringe", we might well be furthering the cause of mainstream science.

"I'm actually quite comfortable with the fact that there's no bright line. I understand why it makes some people antsy, but on the other hand, you also want there to be weird thinking at the edges.

*"Letting stuff float on the fringes is a way of getting new ideas and occasionally sharpening one's critical abilities. During the 1970s, when many fringe doctrines were out there, like Erich von Däniken's Chariots of the Gods or Velikovsky, many science teachers would assign these books to their science classes, saying, "**The assignment for the midterm is to pick a scientific claim in this book and show why it's wrong.**" Then people went out and did research and learned how to make reasoned arguments. That was supposed to be a way of sharpening your teeth."*

It is perhaps worth remembering, too, that Einstein *was* most definitely outside of the scientific mainstream when he had his *annus mirabilis* in 1905 and single-handedly transformed our understanding of nature.

That hardly means that it's going to happen again.

But it might.

The Conversation

I. A Counterculture Hero
Introducing Immanuel Velikovsky

HB: I'm looking forward to talking to you about the distinction between science and pseudoscience and how best to categorize it—indeed, whether it makes any sense at all. But let's start off with the figure of Immanuel Velikovsky. You chose him as an exemplar of the boundary between science and pseudoscience, but you cheerfully admit that most people today wouldn't have any clear idea of who he actually was. So let's just start there. Who was this guy?

MG: One of the reasons why I chose him is precisely because he was once a household name and now is absolutely not: the fact that the story therefore has a distinct end is particularly attractive to me.

But let me start with who he was. He was born in 1895 in the town of Vitebsk, which is now in Belarus, but was then part of the Russian Empire—it's the same town Marc Chagall was from, incidentally.

He comes from a Jewish family and when he's 5 years old, the family moved to Moscow. He eventually gets a medical degree and then the Revolution hits. His family gets out, emigrates to Berlin for a few years and then settles in Palestine. His father buys some apartments in Tel Aviv and Immanuel—the youngest of the three children and the only one who leaves for Tel Aviv with the parents—manages those estates.

He married a violin student while he was in Berlin who moves down to Tel Aviv and they have two daughters. At this point, he's just an ordinary, uninteresting guy.

Slightly more interesting is that after his mother dies he decided that, even though he's trained as a medical doctor (although he doesn't practice), he would like to retrain as a psychoanalyst. So he goes to Vienna for a few years around 1934 and studies psychoanalysis before coming back to Tel Aviv.

At this point he's still pretty uninteresting, historically speaking. But in 1938, he walks by a bookstore and sees a book by Freud. Being a psychoanalyst, he's naturally interested in what Freud had to say. The book is called (in English translation), *Moses and Monotheism*. Velikovsky reads it (in the original German) and he's incensed.

The argument of this book is that Moses is not a Hebrew at all: he's an Egyptian who was a renegade priest within the monotheistic sun god cult of the Pharaoh Akhnaton—a cult which was suppressed very strongly after Akhnaton's death. Moses takes this religion and sells it to the slave population, the Hebrews, who eventually export it from Egypt with Moses. The sun god that they started with gets somehow fused with a Midianite volcano deity associated with Mount Sinai called Jehovah, and that's how modern Judaism emerges.

That's bad enough for Velikovsky, who is raised in a very observant Jewish household and is strongly connected to various religious strands of Zionism, together with secular aspects.

But then it gets even worse.

Because Freud then claims that you can do the same thing you do with dreams to the Bible. That is, what's going on in the Bible is a lot of metaphors and illusions that are like the *dreamwork*, the images we get in dreams. And if you know how to read them right, you can decode the underlying story that this dreamwork is trying to suppress. Freud claims that this underlying story is actually the murder of Moses by the Hebrews who are sick of his puritanical regulations.

This is horrifying to Velikovsky, and he decides he's going to write a refutation of it. He's a psychoanalyst, after all, he says to himself: he can do this. He takes a sabbatical with his family, and they all leave on a steamer to go to New York where he can work in a better library. He arrives in August 1939, settles down in the Upper West Side and goes off to work at the New York Public Library on 42nd Street.

While he's there, he does a great deal of research, and comes to believe that he finds a text, a translation of an Egyptian text that he thinks is the same thing as *Exodus*, just from the Egyptian side. And he says to himself, "*Wow, maybe these events actually happened, but they are not miraculous. What if they were natural disasters? Maybe I can read all of these myths and see if there are homologies between them?*"

Not just analogies, it should be stressed, but actual homologies —that is, stuff that has a common cause. So he reads Chinese myths, Mayan myths, South Asian myths, but mostly Middle Eastern myths, and consistently finds these same things: earthquakes, rocks from heaven, fire from the sky, lightning, massive flooding, and so forth.

So then he concludes, "*There **was** a natural disaster. I can intuit it from global myth, and then I can reverse-engineer things to discover what the global catastrophe actually was*"—using, ironically, the same technique that Freud did with *Moses and Monotheism*.

So he figures it out. In 1950, he publishes it in a book called *Worlds in Collision*, issued by Macmillan Publishers, the leading scientific press in the US at that time; and it rockets to the top of the bestseller lists. It really makes quite a splash. Everybody's discussing it. It's the book of the year. And then about eight weeks into its publication run, Macmillan mysteriously decide that they're going to give it away, they're going to get rid of the book with no cost—just give it to Doubleday, a competitor of theirs.

So then the backstory starts to come out: scientists had written to Macmillan—a few scientists, not that many, about 8-12, saying, "*We are deeply offended that you, a scientific press, published this book*." They describe it as "claptrap", "fictional science", "science fiction", "baloney" and so forth.

HB: Did they use the word "pseudoscience" at that time?

MG: The term "pseudoscience" gets used at various points, but usually not in these first letters—it gets used quite a bit in the reviews of the book that come out later. And once the book appears in April 1950, all the reviews from scientists are extremely negative.

The private letters to Macmillan essentially say, "*We no longer think that you're a reliable press, so we're thinking about boycotting you.*" What that means is not buying their books, not assigning their books to undergraduates (which represents 70 percent of Macmillan's sales), not submitting works for them and not refereeing for Macmillan-related journals.

One of the most articulate of these letters comes in response to an editor who says, "*I want the referee report that you owe me.*" And the scientist responds, "*I'm not going to give it to you. I'm not going to give it to you because you guys published this book.*"

Finally, George Brett, who's the head of Macmillan, says, "*We better not do this.*" So he "de-acquisitions" the book—that's the term I like to use for it. When that becomes public, it becomes this publishing scandal, and many people who enjoyed the book start saying, "*Well, we don't know whether the book is right. Velikovsky thinks it is. But this is like Galileo saying the truth about the heavens and the orthodoxy doesn't want to hear it, and he has been repressed by this homogeneous establishment that doesn't like the fact that he's an outsider giving a new perspective on how things are going on.*"

That makes the book *even more* popular; and for a couple of months, it's still at the top of the bestseller lists. And then it sort of vanishes for a bit. It's dormant for most of the 1950s, but then in the 1960s it gets picked up again, first by a series of acolytes who find it through various nooks and crannies and come to admire the man.

In the meantime, Velikovsky doesn't go back to what is now the state of Israel. In 1952 he moved from New York to settle in Princeton, New Jersey, not far from where we're sitting right now.

And he continues to write more books, many of which are consistent with *Worlds in Collision*. By the mid 1960s the counterculture picks up on it and it once again becomes this huge sensation. Even though Velikovsky is now in his upper 70s, the book comes to speak for the young generation's desire to break out of an established orthodoxy. It is very, very popular throughout the 1970s, and then Velikovsky dies in 1979 and the whole thing kind of crumbles within four or five years.

Today the book is almost unheard of.

Questions for Discussion:

1. Had you heard of **Worlds in Collision** *before? Have you read it?*

2. Is Velikovsky's determination to "write a refutation" of Freud's **Moses and Monotheism** *suspicious to you? To what extent do you think that it prejudices his resulting theories?*

II. An Ideal Case

The historical allure of Velikovsky

MG: So, why am I interested in writing about this? Part of it has to do with the content. Part of it has to do with him. Let me say a bit about him first.

As I said before, I like the fact that the story has a beginning and an end. Velikovsky's life up until about the age of 50 is a completely ordinary and regular one. Then he gets obsessed with this idea, starts to write this book in about 1945 or so, and develops this whole second life.

And then it has an end that's quite distinct. It's rare that you can see a very public fringe doctrine from beginning to end coherently. Other fringe doctrines—creationism, parapsychology, things like that—have much messier beginnings and still continue.

The other part that's relevant to me is that he kept all of his stuff in his house—his fan mail, his hate mail, his drafts and so on —and his widow and daughters gave it to Princeton University Library. It's all sitting here. It's this incredibly well-documented case of a view of a fringe doctrine from the inside: how he thought of it, how it was built up.

HB: And from the outside as well, because you were saying that he collected everything.

MG: Absolutely: he collected everything. He even collected third-party documents. Fans of his would write letters to other people, not admitting that they were Velikovsky supporters so as to get unvarnished reviews, and then gave him the responses. He collected reviews between third parties who aren't supporters, he collected all of the reviews of his book, he collected reviews of books that were like his book, as well as those that weren't. It's an enormously comprehensive archive.

Usually, this sort of stuff gets treated like junk and it gets discarded by the heirs after the person has died. You know the sort of thing: *"That's Uncle Steve. He had this theory about geocentrism. Let's get rid of it."*

But not in this case. And all this is gold for a historian: you can actually see it. So one reason for my interest is the strengths of the documents that exist.

Another reason is the content, which, as a historian of science naturally appeals to me.

Here's this fellow who believes that he can correlate ancient myths. What does he think happened? He thinks that about 1500 BC, which is around the time of the *Exodus* of the children of Israel from Egypt (according to his dating of it), a comet was ejected from the surface of Jupiter.

Now, the idea that comets can be ejected from planets is a live one in astrophysics at that time. At any rate, he claims that some time before then this comet was ejected from Jupiter, and then around 1500 BC it comes hurtling towards earth.

It gets trapped in a sort of gravitational and—importantly for him—electromagnetic union with the earth, and there are lightning bolts coming from this comet to earth. The earth rumbles, its axis tilts and slows down a little bit, the crust fractures: all sorts of bad things happen.

The comet doesn't get within the limit (the so-called Roche limit) whereby it will crack up because of tidal pressures, but it's out there and it's very, very visible: it's the most dominant thing in the sky.

And after about 50 years of this, it somehow breaks off and settles down into a regular orbit around the sun and becomes Venus— our closest planetary neighbour, second planet from the sun. In a nutshell: the birth of Venus is such that humanity not only witnessed it, but witnessed it once people had already developed writing.

People put down the story in many texts, but it was so traumatic and so incredibly devastating that they encoded it as myth, which was the way that they could understand it—as miracles, divine intervention, something like that.

But, in fact, the whole thing was just a natural phenomenon of the rearrangement of the solar system. Venus also happens to displace Mars, and Mars threatens Earth in a second bout that happens around 800 BC, and then Mars settles down in its current orbit around the sun.

So Velikovsky gives us this new theory of the solar system. Instead of being derived from statistical mechanics or astronomical observations, it's derived from what he considers to be *eyewitness testimony*: people who were *actually there*, saw it and gave us this information—but the information is spotty and encoded and you need to learn how to decode it.

In order to decode it, he uses some ancient astronomical data from the Babylonians, he uses a lot of mythological data, and then he uses a lot of historical data about king lists in Egypt and so on to get the timing to work out right.

But the central point is that you have these two massive catastrophes. I thought this idea was fascinating. It's an amazing fusion of an obsession with ancient history, world religions and the cosmos, and it touches the physical sciences very deeply.

Most of these fringe doctrines that one hears about have to do with biology or geology, but very few have to do with astronomy—aside from astrology, which is a separate, much more fraught case. Here is something that was publicly available, very widely discussed and extremely exciting to a lot of different people.

For my part, I wanted to figure out how we got there, together with why the scientific community reacted so strongly, so quickly. There are many cases in the history of science like phrenology—the idea that the bumps on your head determine your personality—or Mesmerism—an invisible natural force that animals exert—that start out as plausible, then there's a debate and then it gets kicked out.

But here, there was no debate. This got kicked out instantly, yet still lived on, continuing to live in this zone where people consistently called it *pseudoscientific*. What finally made it go away was not the scientists battling against it in 1950 or the 1970s, but simply that the leader of the movement dies and the energy associated with it peters out.

Questions for Discussion:

1. Why do you think that Michael regards astrology as a "separate, much more fraught case"? What do you think he means by this, exactly?

2. Have theories like phrenology or mesmerism left any sort of mark on current scientific thinking?

III. The Lysenko Lesson
Science meets politics

HB: An obvious question is why the scientific community reacted as strongly as it did to Velikovsky in 1950. In your book, you highlight the Lysenko case of 1948 as a key precursor, in terms of an understanding amongst scientists as to what should be done about crazy guys promoting crazy theories. Let's talk a bit about that.

MG: Actually, this is part of a historical puzzle that got me moving in this direction in the first place. Some time ago, someone asked me, *"Would you be interested in writing a book on pseudoscience?"* And I said, "Well, it's a very problematic category and I'm not sure. Let me look at it." I started picking up a few cases and doing some reading. Velikovsky was going to be one of those cases.

I was talking with a student in my office about what I was reading, and it suddenly occurred to me that all of these different cases happened in the early 1950s. That's puzzling, because weird theories appear constantly, many times a day, everywhere. The vast majority of them sink without a trace. No one says anything.

What's interesting about Velikovsky is that it didn't sink without a trace. It could have been ignored, it could have gotten two negative reviews, and everyone would've said, *"It's a flash in the pan. It'll go away."* Scientists are busy people. They have lots of things to do and they can't investigate or debunk every strange theory that comes their way.

HB: And there's also the danger that it might backfire. You might not want to give added press to something.

MG: Exactly. Escalating it to the point of a public campaign against something is a very bold move, and you would only do that if you're willing to invest the time and the energy against all those risks to do so.

The question, then, is why around 1950 do you see this happening in multiple different areas? Velikovsky is the biggest case, but by no means the only one—L. Ron Hubbard's *Dianetics* is also published in 1950 and gets some similar press, in the same way, from the psychological community. So, why?

In the early 20th century, there's very little of this kind of stuff. There's the Scopes Trial about creationism and there are a couple of other moments, but they don't have this kind of scale.

So it must have something to do with this particular moment of the late 1940s. I think that there are two parts to that. The Lysenko case is part two. Part one is that, in 1945, physics had suddenly changed. Physics used to be a relatively small field, a couple thousand people worldwide (meaning North America, Europe and a couple in South America and East Asia). But after World War II, they're the single best-funded, most visible, community of scientists the world has ever seen.

They get an enormous amount of funding, power and scrutiny— and this is a moment when there's a tremendous amount of scrutiny by the House Un-American Activities Committee, and eventually by Senator McCarthy, about these *"egg-head scientists who can make very serious weapons."* The Soviets also have some of these people. So it's a moment of tremendous anxiety for this particular community, and anxiety is crucial.

HB: They're under the microscope.

MG: Absolutely. If you look at who gets hauled before the House Un-American Activities Committee, there are many actors and union leaders and so on. But among scientists, it's overwhelmingly and disproportionately physicists—and not just physicists, but theoretical physicists. There's one experimentalist: Frank Oppenheimer, the brother of J. Robert, but that's it.

That's striking: that among physicists—who are the overwhelming scientific group—theoretical physicists are dominant, because they are seen to be having something to do with the bomb. So the microscope is there and the stakes are quite high: you can be blacklisted, you can be fired. This is the time when David Bohm leaves for Sao Paolo. It's not a good scene.

So there's a lot of anxiety about this. And then something happens in the Soviet Union—this is part two—that makes things come to a head in mid-1948. It's the reverberations of that, I think, that trigger the reaction to Velikovsky in 1950.

In the Soviet Union, there's a man named Trofim Denisovich Lysenko, who is an agronomist. Starting in the late 1920s, he performed a fair number of small-scale experiments with very equivocal results, but he comes to believe that particulate inheritance in the form of genes—which is then the dominant, but not the overwhelmingly dominant, theory—isn't true; and that instead some kind of modified inheritance of acquired characteristics is how heredity actually happens.

HB: Right. We should stress that this is before DNA was discovered.

MG: Yes. The discovery of the structure of DNA happens in 1953. At the time, most people who think about heredity are geneticists of some form, but they sometimes allow for some of what's called "soft heredity", which means the possibility of some impact of the environment on inheritance.

But Lysenko argues that he can transform species from one kind to another by taking a seed and rubbing it with ice. He calls this "vernalization". Some of these techniques have been around since the 1860s: they're very common agronomical techniques that plant physiologists were interested in, but he thinks they have implications for heredity.

In the 1930s he links it up with Marxist ideology and Stalin gets interested in this as an alternative to the geneticists. This is the same moment when the Nazis are using genetics for very different kinds of political claims, so having an alternative seems like a good idea.

Not just the Nazis, I should add: there are Americans who are also prominently making the same sort of eugenic arguments.

Anyway, Lysenko has this moment where he struggles with the genetics establishment. After World War II, the struggle continues (it pretty well goes on hiatus during the war). In 1948 it looks like there's going to be some discussion either way about how this is going to go. There's a meeting of the Lenin All-Union Academy of Agricultural Sciences, of which Lysenko is now the president (since the late 1930s), and he gives a speech with all of his usual arguments—inheritance through acquired characteristics, Soviet Darwinism, genes are pseudoscientific and bourgeois—and his last lines are *"The central committee has read this report and approved it,"* which means that Stalin has approved it.

In fact, now we know better than that: we actually know that Stalin line-edited the report and in fact took out some of the more inflammatory stuff. Stalin toned it down. But the report's very toned-up as you look at it: the upshot is that it's illegal to practice genetics in the Soviet Union. And it stays that way until 1965.

There is some genetics being done as radiation biology under the protection of nuclear physicists, but it almost wipes out the entire field. And this is a global scandal. It becomes propagated as a new Soviet science and the Eastern block and China start to adopt aspects of it after 1949 when the People's Republic of China is established.

It becomes this way of dividing the biological world into two camps, and communist parties in England and France have to take positions on the matter.

In the US it gets a very particular reaction from geneticists who say, *"Well, earlier we had not liked Lysenko, we thought he was a problematic guy. But we thought we could argue with him in a debate among scientists. Politics should stay out of it—especially anti-Soviet claims, which might make the state back Lysenko more. We should make it all about science."*

After 1948, they say, *"The state has spoken and this is now no longer science. It's outside the realm of science."*

It's not even in the spectrum of "excellent science-good science-OK science-bad science-really bad science". At first, they thought it was really bad science. Now they think it's right off the grid: it's pseudoscience. And suddenly, that term gets bandied around much more in 1948.

HB: You wrote about two guys in particular who were worried that the whole issue would simply become a political football, thrown into the McCarthyist winds and used as a source of leverage to damn the Soviet Union holus-bolus. They say, "*Let's try another way. Let's soft-peddle this. Let's not publicly condemn this stuff, but, in fact, try to bring it into the public scientific discourse.*" And one of these guys actually translated Lysenko's work, if I remember correctly.

MG: Right. One of these people is Theodosius Dobzhansky, who is most famous for having written *Genetics and the Origin of Species*, which is the first book in 1937 that actually tries to unify the Mendelian line and the Darwinian positions. He's one of the more important evolutionary theorists of the 20th century, but he's also Russian-born (Ukrainian-born, actually), and translated Lysenko into English in a very calm way, precisely so that people could have a scientific discussion about it and then reject it.

The other important character here is Leslie Clarence Dunn. They're both at Columbia. The reason I can track what is happening is that they write letters to each other all the time, which is quite puzzling at first, because you ask yourself, "*They're in the same department, why are they doing this?*"

Well, it's because Dobzhansky is travelling around collecting samples in Brazil, so there's this discussion happening by letters over time. One of the wonderful things about this period is that people wrote letters, and the mail came twice per day, so you can see the evolution of their thoughts over a very specific period of time.

Dunn, in particular, is involved in US-Soviet scientific cooperation, an attempt to try to avert a cold war by keeping the intellectuals talking to each other. And, in fact, when the scientists bring out the pseudoscience arguments in 1948 or so, it *does* get picked up by the anti-communists and the right wing as evidence that the Soviet Union is an irrational place that can't do science, and only democratic societies can have science.

Part of the reason why that political stuff matters is that when you look at who the leaders or the most prominent people against Velikovsky are, they're all left-liberal people. They're all people who are not communists, by any means, but they are liberal and not anti-Soviet. They're moderately pro-Soviet in terms of how foreign policy should work.

So they want to condemn Lysenko, but they want to further generalize by saying, "*Well, we're not just condemning Lysenko, we're condemning all of these kinds of bad sciences. Look here's one by a guy who's citing the Bible and lots of religious texts: he's kind of like a right-wing guy and we can attack him too on the same grounds.*"

First of all, they come to believe that crackpots can be very, very dangerous; but secondly, they think they can shore up their liberal credentials by saying, "*We condemned Lysenko, but we can also condemn this guy.*"

Questions for Discussion:

1. Is scientific activity more, less, or just as politicized today as it was in 1950?

2. Why does Michael mention David Bohm? Who was he and why did he leave for Brazil?

IV. A Freudian Cosmology
Validation by hostility

HB: So now there's no reason for any scientist not to promptly and vociferously attack Velikovsky, because there are political reasons to have a balance in targets, and they can say, "*We tried the 'Let's bring this into the public scientific consciousness and have a debate' method before, and that didn't work—look what happened.*"

MG: Right. I would expect that if you had a time machine and went back and asked scientists in 1952 or 1953 what they thought about the way they reacted to *Worlds In Collision* when it came out in 1950, they would say, "*Oh, we shouldn't have condemned the book the way that we did because it made it very popular.*"

It's possible that it would have been popular as it was, but they didn't just help make it more popular because everybody loves a scandal and this is the *succès de scandale* of the year, and it also gave a persecution narrative to the story.

It could have been a debate about many things. It could have been a debate about crossing fields and what happens when someone from psychology moves into geophysics or astronomy. It could have been about science and religion—which is, I think, what many people thought it was going to be about when it began. But instead it becomes about Galileo.

HB: The modern-day Galileo.

MG: Yes. The "New Galileo Affair". In fact, it began to be called the "Velikovsky Affair" precisely for the same reason. That's part of the appeal, it's part of the fuel that keeps the "Velikovsky industry" going well into the future when the counterculture gets drawn in: this narrative of persecution by the authorities.

HB: There seem to be many ironies here, but one particular one that struck me concerns the very genesis of the work. Here is this psychoanalyst who starts out by setting out to rebut Freud's *Moses and Monotheism*, and in so doing he develops a theory that is a mixture of history and science: taking the historical, religious documents seriously as witness testimony, smoking guns of scientific evidence for his claims.

But then, as you described in your book, he goes on to talk in Freudian terms about the persecution that he is receiving by the scientific community.

MG: Absolutely.

HB: He says words to the effect of, *"In the common history of humanity, we've suffered this incredible shock that we have long been suppressing, and what I am doing now is making people come to terms with this. But given the trauma that we've suffered, it's entirely natural that people would reject this message, so their reaction of suppression and persecution that I'm a victim of is entirely understandable."*

MG: Yes. It's Freudian all the way through.

In this view, the neurosis that we first had was encapsulated by Aristotelianism: an attempt to try and find an order in the universe. Science, as a whole, is obsessed with the idea that the universe is ordered; and the reason why we feel compelled to do that is because the universe was disordered at one point, and it almost killed us.

So, this uniformitarian idea—the idea that the same laws of physics that work now have always been working, that the solar system has basically always been this way, say—is viewed as a manifestation of this neurosis.

He wants to write a book refuting Freud, but that's not because he is opposed to Freudianism: he is psychoanalytic all the way through.

The two threads that go throughout his entire life are a particular interpretation of Zionism, and Freudianism of some form or other. The book that he was originally going to write about Freud was designed to be in three parts.

The first part is a reanalysis of Freud's dreams. Freud famously made a big splash with the book *The Interpretation of Dreams* in 1899. In it there are six dreams that Freud says are his, for which he gives an interpretation. Velikovsky says, *"Those interpretations are wrong. I can reinterpret them better. They're all about a self-hating Jewish individual worrying about conversion."*

The second part is going to be about Oedipus, the central myth for Freud. Velikovsky had this theory that Oedipus and Akhnaton, who was another one of Freud's avatars, are the same person. You can use the history to help reinterpret the Oedipus myth, and you can use the Oedipus myth to help re-interpret the history of Egypt.

Why, for example, is it Thebes—which happens to be a city in both Egypt and in Greece—where Oedipus travels to and becomes king? Why is it a Sphinx, of all things, that he meets along the way?

So part two is going to be called *Freud and His Heroes*, and that segment eventually gets published as *Oedipus and Akhnaton: Myth and History* in 1960. It's an amazing book, completely worth reading. Just like *Worlds in Collision*, Velikovsky takes the myths to interpret the science and the science to interpret the myths, and there's always a risk of circularity: it's never quite clear which one is the dependent variable.

The third part is going to be about Moses, but he doesn't know what he's going to do with it exactly. It's researching this Moses part that gets him to *Worlds in Collision*.

I should say that, in the process, he also has to reinterpret all of ancient history, because to combine the Egyptian text that he thinks corroborates the stories from *Exodus*, he has to erase eight centuries of Egyptian history. The way he does this is by mapping different Egyptian kings on to each other. Egyptian kings often have several names, and he claims that some of these people we think of as two different pharaohs are actually two names of the same pharaoh.

It's somewhat analogous to saying, "*Barbarossa and Winston Churchill are pretty well the same.*" and, "*World War I looks a lot like the Thirty Years' War; and that's because they're the same war. They're just displaced by several centuries.*"

Those are my analogies, of course, not Velikovsky's. But those who criticize him make arguments like that.

But throughout, he never gives up the Freudian explanation. The ideas of amnesia and repression saturate his understanding of the world very, very deeply, while giving him a ready-made way of explaining the reaction to his work.

In the end, he comes to believe that there *had* to have been a "Velikovsky Affair", because if he was right, this event should be so traumatic that it *must* still produce this reaction. In other words, the very hostility of the scientific community towards him becomes evidence in favour of the theory.

Questions for Discussion:

1. Is it possible that our strong belief in the existence of "the laws of nature" is more reflective of our primal fears and desires than a product of objective facts?

2. To what extent is Freudianism compatible with the scientific method?

V. Enter Einstein
Velikovsky makes predictions

HB: Velikovsky seems to be doing this sort of thing all the time: claiming evidence for his theory based upon what's already happened. That's the classic argument made when accusing someone of engaging in pseudoscience—scientists often accuse economists of this sort of thing—"*Your theory never actually predicts anything. You simply retrodict whatever happens within your theory while saying, 'Of course my theory said it had to be that way'.*"

MG: Yes: everything becomes a confirming instance, and that type of debate becomes a pretty important strand within the philosophy of science. Hopefully we'll get back to that.

HB: I'm sure we will. But now back to the Velikovsky story. So he published *Worlds in Collision* in 1950...

MG: Right. He moves to Princeton in 1952 and he lives right by the lake that people row on here. In 1953 he sees a guy get out of a rowboat kind of in front of his house. It's Albert Einstein, the most famous person who lives in Princeton.

Einstein doesn't remember that they'd met before in the 1920s. They also met again in the mid-1940s when Velikovsky took the train down to Princeton to talk his theory through, and Einstein told him, "*Don't publish this.*"

But Velikovsky *did* publish it, of course, and Einstein became very angry about it, so he wants nothing more to do with Velikovsky. But eventually they start to chat, mostly because Einstein's secretary and his stepdaughter persuade him that he should listen to this guy.

So they have a lot of discussions, and one of the things Einstein says to him is, "*Look, what you're doing is not scientific. But what **would** be scientific is if you actually make some predictions.*"

So Velikovsky goes on a quest through *Worlds in Collision*, asking himself, "*What are my predictions?*"

"*Well, I predict that Venus should be hot, because it's incandescent: it just burst from Jupiter, so it should be warm.*" Most people at that time thought Venus was probably cold, like Mars or the Moon. Venus is actually a weird planet. It spins the opposite way from all the other planets, and it has a nearly perfect circular orbit, which is actually not good for Velikovsky's argument. Anyway, Venus should be warm—that's the first prediction he makes.

The second prediction is that Jupiter should emit radio noises. Now, Jupiter's cold; it shouldn't do that, but he thinks it should because it's electromagnetically active.

And thirdly, he thinks that the atmosphere of Venus should have hydrocarbons in it. He thinks that's why the flames came down to earth, because the hydrocarbon-rich atmosphere of Venus left traces on earth and deposited large amounts of crude oil on the planet. A large part of the book is about the ratio of carbohydrates versus hydrocarbons. At any rate, according to Velikovsky, there should have been some exchange of atmospheres, so we can reverse-engineer what the atmosphere of Venus should be like.

Those are his three predictions.

It turns out that Venus *is* actually warm. We now say it's warm because of planetary atmosphere and the greenhouse effect. Incidentally, the planetary atmosphere of Venus was the topic of specialization of Carl Sagan, who becomes one of the most visible anti-Velikovskians in the 1970s.

The second prediction, radio signals from Jupiter, is discovered in 1955, and Einstein is very impressed by it. He says, "*Wow, I guess you actually **did** predict that.*" And then he adds, "*Because you predicted that successfully, I'm going to write a letter for whatever test of your theory that you want.*"

And what Velikovsky asks for is to do carbon dating on an Egyptian mummy to figure out whether his dating scheme is correct—carbon dating was first proposed by Willard Libby in 1946, and confirmed in 1949.

But Einstein dies in the spring of 1955 before he gets a chance to write the letter, and Velikovsky has the letter written by Helen Dukas, Einstein's longtime secretary.

The third prediction, hydrocarbons on Venus, is a more complicated story. At the beginning of the space age, when the first probes go by Venus and start studying its atmosphere, they find some carbon in the atmosphere.

But NASA didn't want to publicly say "organic compounds", because they were worried that people would immediately conclude that they had found life there. So during a press conference, one of the NASA spokespeople people instead said they had found "hydrocarbons".

Now it turns out that that's a misinterpretation of the evidence and it's not actually true. But when he said "hydrocarbons", the Velikovskians—who aren't many, but are quite loud—announced, *"We've been confirmed by modern technology. Velikovsky made predictions based on these ancient texts that turn out to be verifiably true, now that we can actually do space-age stuff. So this ancient knowledge is future knowledge."*

Prediction, then, becomes a very important part of the story of Velikovsky constantly trying to get himself accepted by the scientific establishment. It should be stressed that Velikovsky believes, like virtually all people who are labeled pseudo-scientific, that he's acting like a real scientist.

Velikovsky thinks he's doing science. He comes to appreciate that scientists are supposed to make predictions, so he does too. And when they're confirmed he wants to be accepted.

There's a lot of discussion about these particular claims. There's a letter to the editor in *Science* from two very distinguished scientists, Lloyd Motz at Columbia and Valentine Bargmann at Princeton, effectively saying, *"Give the guy a hearing. He did actually predict some stuff. Maybe we should do some tests."*

Questions for Discussion:

1. Why do you think the fact that Venus has an almost perfectly circular orbit is "not good for Velikovsky's argument"?

2. Why do you think Einstein was more impressed by the confirmation of radio waves from Jupiter than the confirmed prediction that Venus should be warm? To what extent are some confirmed predictions "more meaningful" than others?

VI. Responses and Reactions
Publicity and hostility

HB: You say that he thinks he's doing science, but you also write about how he referred to himself as a historian rather than as a scientist.

MG: Yes, absolutely.

HB: So that's not to say that he didn't think he was doing science, but he seemed to value himself first and foremost as a historian. But he wasn't accepted by the historical community, either.

MG: No, that's right. He makes scientific claims, but he does think of his identity primarily as a historian, because that's his method. His method was to look through ancient texts and interpret what happened. This led him to a reinterpretation of science, but fundamentally he believes that he's a historian.

The reception of Velikovsky by the astronomers and the physicists versus the historians is an excellent contrast. The physicists get very, very upset about it. When it comes to history, in many ways, what he's suggesting is much more transformative still: he thinks the chronology is all backwards and centuries should be rejected, that they're reading the texts all wrong, and so forth. But the historians essentially completely ignore him.

There are a couple of reviews, which say, "*No one should bother reading this.*" But there's no "history war". There's no discussion about this throughout the field of history. It just drops like a stone.

The historians aren't in a particular position of anxiety in that period. They don't feel any need to combat it. They get things like this all the time in the ancient world, so they just let it go.

So instead of *Worlds in Collision* being regarded as a history book with some science claims, it becomes a science book with some history claims. The scientists' reaction channels it in the direction of science, when it might have been channelled differently.

HB: How much of that is because of the way it came out? At the beginning of our conversation you described how Macmillan Publishing eventually withdrew it from their collection under a storm of protest from scientists and gave away the rights to Doubleday.

You also mentioned that a core market for Macmillan—which presumably strongly influenced their decision—was science textbooks. Perhaps another way to look at this is that historians might have reacted differently had Macmillan been primarily distributing history textbooks.

MG: It could very well have been. Velikovsky shopped it to eight different publishers, and the first one that bit was Macmillan. The original book was called *Exodus in Exile*, which combined the history arguments and science arguments.

And an editor at Macmillan named James Putnam said, "*We'll take it. We'll publish it all, but we want you to separate things so that we'll publish the science stuff first and we'll publish the history stuff later.*"

In other words, yes: a part of the eventual reaction is probably the press channelling it that way. And at the beginning of *Worlds in Collision* Velikovsky writes, "*The history argument is essential to understanding why I think all these texts are referring to the same incident. But that will come later. Just assume that I've proved that for now.*"

Part of what happened, then, is likely attributable to the way the press produced it, while another part is how it was received by the respective academic communities.

When something like this happens, the immediate reaction someone today would have would be, "*Well, it must not have been peer-reviewed, because no one would have approved this.*"

Well peer review is a much more recent phenomenon than many people tend to assume. *Nature* didn't, as a matter of course, have regularly peer-reviewed papers until the 1970s. *Physical Review* only started submitting all its articles to peer review after World War II. They peer-reviewed some earlier, and you can find elements of peer review in the 19th century, but it wasn't routine.

At any rate, *Worlds in Collision* **was** actually submitted to peer review twice: two sets of three reviewers. All of them clear it, but what they say is interesting.

They effectively say, "*Okay, so this book's not right. But it's* **interesting**, *and it'll probably sell because it's well written and has exciting stories in it. It might spark some discussion about science, religion and history. So, publish it, by all means. I think it will be good for you.*"

What they believe peer review to be all about is not vouchsafing the veracity of a text, but rather giving advice to the publisher about what's worth publishing and what's not based on the publisher's criteria—not the scientific community's criteria.

Because of many diverse incidents, Velikovsky's being one of them, peer review starts to mean something rather different: it comes to be about gate-keeping and keeping out stuff that's not supposed to be out there.

But all those people who review *Worlds in Collision* are scientists or science writers. Macmillan wanted to frame it as a science book, in part because they believe that science will sell better than an ancient history book.

HB: And some of the reviewers, if I remember correctly, wound up paying dearly for their early endorsements of Velikovsky's book.

MG: Yes. The first round of reviews is all by science writers and presenters of science to the public. One of them, Gordon Atwater, was Director of the Hayden Planetarium at the Museum of Natural History in New York.

HB: Neil deGrasse Tyson's predecessor.

MG: Yes, exactly: distant predecessor. At any rate, Atwater wrote a review of the book, saying essentially, "*Yeah, it's probably not right.*

But it's interesting." And, in his review, he explicitly says, *"I'm the director of a planetarium, and I would like to do a show about this so that people can learn about the solar system using Velikovsky's story about Venus as a narrative. We can discuss whether it's right or wrong and have all sides of the discussion present: it will be a way of educating people."*

HB: Again, there were this driving motivation of bringing science into the public consciousness, getting people excited and interested in discussing the ideas.

MG: Exactly. That's one of science's missions. And the thing is, that mission often conflicts with the gate-keeping mission, not only because certain kinds of simplifications happen, but also because some sensational things that people want to talk about and hear about—

HB:—are just nonsense.

MG: Yes: they don't pass muster. Well, Atwater had gotten this job as kind of a patronage post because he was a naval navigator who taught navigation to the troops during World War II, which he did in New York at the planetarium—it was an easy way to train large officer corps. Then he got the job as director of the planetarium after the war was over.

And then he got fired from the job. He wrote a review or summary of *Worlds in Collision* for a periodical called *This Week*, which is like *Parade*—it was in all the newspapers. The trustees got wind of it, and before the piece even appeared, they said, *"Pack up your office. We'll pay you six months' severance, but you need to resign now."*

He never got a job in science again and grew increasingly embittered over time. There are a good many letters between Atwater and Velikovsky, especially when certain acolytes of Velikovsky get interested in reviving the persecution narrative: they go back and ask Atwater what happened, exactly.

By the way, that Macmillan editor I mentioned earlier, James Putnam, also got fired, but the claim at the time was that there were many different reasons for his dismissal.

Questions for Discussion:

1. Do you think that Gordon Atwater deserved to be fired from his position at the Hayden Planetarium based upon his actions as described in this chapter?

2. Should there be a difference between peer review for a scientific journal and peer review for a commercial press? Should a commercial press even necessarily engage in a peer-review process at all?

VII. Digging In
Unorthodox, up to a point

HB: I want to abstract away from Velikovsky in a bit, but before I do, it's probably worth pointing out that, aside altogether from his theories and the reactions to them and all that, this guy comes across as a really fascinating person.

First of all, he seems to be someone with unlimited amounts of energy. Just the idea that he's able to go into the library and collect all this data and build a narrative and vigorously defend it—he seems to be somebody who just has energy coming out of every possible pore. He's a real character. I can imagine Einstein being repeatedly bothered and harassed by Velikovsky, but eventually coming to think, *"This guy is probably crazy, but he's an entertaining fellow to have around."* Einstein, of course, had a large anti-conformist streak himself, and he probably had a certain respect for Velikovsky's independent spirit.

MG: And Velikovsky's a Zionist, which has a certain appeal for Einstein.

HB: Right. But at any rate, you certainly get this sense of him being an incredibly colourful character. You have to tip your hat to his work ethic, if nothing else. He really seems like a fascinating figure.

MG: Absolutely. Again, he's 50 before he even starts writing his major work. The only other person I can think of with this much energy, and a complete turnaround in his career, is Ivan Pavlov. Pavlov had a scientific career for which he won the Nobel Prize; and then another, separate, scientific career—all the psychology stuff—and does most of his advanced work after 65.

The energy is quite amazing. Because Velikovsky lived in this town, I've talked to several people who have met him. You can watch various YouTube videos of him—there were two documentaries, a BBC and a CBC documentary made of him while he was still alive—and they show him giving lectures to college audiences when he's in his 80s. It doesn't come across there, but he's very tall and everyone mentions these very penetrating eyes, like seeing through you—very charismatic, very engaged. When he talks about his work, it's so clear that he's sincere. He's so convinced himself that he can convince you.

In the inner circle, there's a lot of prickliness associated with that—that's often true with charismatic people—but there are many reasons why this guy just stands out. You can see why he was so popular on college campuses, why people were so persuaded by him, why some of them moved to the area so that they could come and visit him on Hartley Avenue more regularly. Many of them kept up long correspondences with him.

HB: This brings up another point you mentioned in your book. As you said, he first tried to have his theories accepted by the scientific community, but was rebuffed. He tried to have his ideas accepted by the historical community, but was rebuffed again. Eventually he was able to establish his own network outside of the mainstream.

There were Velikovskian journals, Velikovskian supporters in the media, and so forth. But then the following issue arises: once you set up your own camp, you have to vigilantly protect the orthodoxy within that particular camp.

Larger questions inevitably arose about how to maintain discipline within his own troops. Some people are hurling epithets at him like, *"What you're doing to me, because I'm coming up with some variation on the theory, is exactly what people had done to you, in terms of censorship or in terms of forcing you to conform!"*

So you get this interesting sociological effect, which presumably happens with anybody who sets up their camp outside of an established area.

MG: Yes. There's a kind of fractal quality of this: at each layer you go it seems to replicate itself. In the book, I call this "mimesis". Velikovsky says, *"Okay, I'm a scientist of some kind. I'm a historian. I'm a scholar. What do I do? I do what other people do."*

Then, when you're not accepted by the establishment, you try to figure out new ways to persuade them. If those don't work, and you're convinced that you're right, then you need to have a research program. So you develop a research program. Then you need a foundation, or some other way of funding those particular research projects. He gets a couple of angels who are interested in funding that. He has a research assistantship: someone donates the money and an undergraduate from Princeton becomes his RA (research assistant), or, in many cases, a high school kid gets a subsidy to live in his house during the summer and help file his papers.

You create journals with the same structures as others—a kind of peer review, but the peer review is all done by people who are Velikovskians. But then again, particle physicists would not send their work to a biologist to get it peer-reviewed.

You replicate the same structures as any other community. Now what does every scientific community do? They guard their borders. You might think that if you're on the fringe yourself you'd be more tolerant of creationists or parapsychologists or what have you, but in fact, you actually have to be quite worried that their theory is going to make you look bad, so you have to be careful to distinguish yourself from them.

You're something distinct; and when they try to blur the borders or push you further out to the fringe, you need to be very aggressive about maintaining your status.

Part of the reason you don't see that aggression the same way in neurobiology labs, say, is because they're so close to the centre that there's no risk of them being completely fringed out.

Within the mainstream you can have disagreements, fundamental conceptual disagreements that go on for decades, in a somewhat hostile but not, *"You're a crank and a crackpot"* kind of way.

But on the fringe, any question of your legitimacy is so sensitive because you're clinging on by your fingernails. You have to be much more aggressive about it. Whenever anybody tries to cross over and do a little creationism and a little Velikovsky at once, Velikovsky can't tolerate it. And the creationists can't tolerate it either.

Everybody on the fringe thinks that everybody else is pseudo and **they're** the legitimate path. That's a very common phenomenon. You see this in any area that's slightly edgy, because anytime you want to make certain claims about the brain, or certain claims about social psychology, or claims that have a parallel claim that looks like it but is kooky, you have to be very, very careful about precision.

Questions for Discussion:

1. To what extent is the concept of "charisma" compatible with the notion of scientific proof?

2. Why does Michael use the word "fractal"? What is a fractal and how is it related to his notion of "mimesis"?

VIII. Science vs. Pseudoscience
In search of a bright line

HB: If I'm somebody who doesn't have a scientific background at all, I can imagine listening to all of this and saying, "*Maybe all of these claims are just the same in principle and it just depends on how big your army is, on how big your propaganda machine is? Maybe there's **no** objective difference between what we call "science" and what we call "pseudoscience"? Tell me what the line of demarcation is, Michael. Give me a clear way of determining the difference between science and pseudoscience, because if that's not possible, then everything is all the same.*"

MG: Let me break that into a few parts. There's the question, "Is everything actually all the same if there's no strict line of demarcation?" I'll set that aside for a second.

The question about a clear line of demarcation between science and pseudoscience has a very long history, right back to the earliest writings about science in the Western tradition.

The Hippocratic corpus has this text in it called *On the Sacred Disease*. It's from 400 BC, or so. The sacred disease is also known as the "falling sickness", which today we would call epilepsy. Hippocrates has an explanation for what epilepsy is, and it's not the one that we believe now, but what he's worried about are these witch doctors and faith healers. Those people, he believes, they're terrible. So from the very beginning of the Western scientific tradition, this "border thing" has been an issue. It's always an issue whenever you're trying to guard your terrain.

People have thus long been looking for a decision procedure: *How can we tell?* But the problem is, there's no way to tell *ex ante*.

You can always tell *ex post*, you can always look back and say, "*Oh well, **that** theory isn't confirmable. It doesn't actually have any evidence, or it's logically inconsistent, or it doesn't explain as much as this other theory which is consistent with all these other theories we have.*"

HB: But once you have a theory that works—

MG: Then you can simply say, "*Well, it works.*" Or if you're not quite sure a theory works, but it seems plausible, then you can keep things in play for a long time.

There were lots of variants of atomism or anti-atomism that were at play in the 19th century. No one was quite sure which one was right, and for about 60–70 years people just let them all be, waiting to see what would happen.

The bright line of demarcation between science and non-science is an issue that people have long been very concerned about. The one individual people usually point to who began systematizing work on this is Karl Popper.

In the 1950s, he gave a lecture that became a canonical source for people interested in what he called "the demarcation problem"—that's where the term gets its name. The story goes that in 1919 Popper was wandering through Vienna and became very impressed with news of the eclipse expedition that confirmed Einstein's general theory of relativity. In particular, he was impressed that Einstein risks something.

Einstein said, "*Light bends around stars. It bends this much. Go ahead and look. If it doesn't, I'm wrong.*" Einstein's actual views about how the experiment would work are more nuanced than that, but that doesn't matter here. This is Popper's public presentation.

In a sense, it's a very masculinist way of thinking, like gambling. The fact that Einstein risks everything is what makes him scientific. For Popper, this is contrasted with three things he sees around him in Vienna: scientific socialism—Marxist theories of history, Freud's theories of psychoanalysis and Adler's theories of psychology about inferiority complexes and so forth.

What bothers him about all of these is that they don't risk anything. Suppose there's a claim such as, "**This** is what causes homosexuality." But if you were to point out, "*Here's someone who had that experience but **isn't** homosexual*," they would simply respond with something like, "*Well, but he's latent*," or, "*That's because he has this other thing which neutralizes the first thing*."

HB: This gets back to my early comments about economists...

MG: Absolutely: it's confirmation bias. Now, the dominant philosophical school in Vienna at that time is Logical Positivism, which had a very strong tradition of verificationism: that is, science is science because it finds things that verify itself against nature. Popper thinks that's not true, because he believes that one can always find verifying instances, or at least interpret them as verifying instances.

What he wanted instead is what he came to call "falsificationism". He says, "Something is scientific when it says, '*If you find this, I'm wrong*'." In other words, *It's not about being **right**. It's about **not being wrong yet**.*

It's very appealing. I often get this quoted to me by undergraduates who don't see why I'm so exercised about this question of demarcation. They say, "*Look, it's simple: falsifiability.*"

HB: Not just undergraduates, by the way. Many professional scientists will unhesitatingly say that too.

MG: Yes. It's a very appealing criterion. Except it's got a couple of problems.

Problem one is, *How do you know that you falsified something?* If it were the case that every time an experiment with a null result meant that you'd falsified something, then everything we know about physics and chemistry will be wrong because high school students around the world have failed to replicate it. So you have to do the experiment *right*.

But how do you know you've done the experiment "right", unless you get "the right result"? This is something sociologists call "the experimenter's regress": you really need to figure out some way of breaking that cycle. How do you know you've done the experiment right but gotten a null result? So that's one particular problem that can be very, very touchy in lots of cases.

HB: Again, as we were saying earlier, there's a quote by Einstein, which could certainly be apocryphal, but in this case I don't think it is. Apparently when somebody asked him about the 1919 test of General Relativity, *"What if they hadn't actually got this result?"*, he replied—

MG: *"I'd be sorry for the dear Lord: the theory is correct."* Yes, exactly. I think that quote *is*, actually, apocryphal, but I think it's consistent with a lot of things Einstein would have said.

As it happens, there's a clear case of this involving Special Relativity, which made predictions about the measurements of electrons. There was a series of experiments by Walter Kaufmann, where he measured these things and didn't get Einstein's result; and Einstein said that something must be wrong with the experiment.

HB: And something was.

MG: Yes, something was; but it took them three *years* to find it. Which means that for a long time, Einstein was simply denying this experiment. So it's very, very tricky to determine when that happens. Anyway, that's problem one.

Problem two is that any valuable demarcation criterion has to cut the world in the right place. That is, we want to make sure that all the things that we regard as science are scientific, and those things that we think as "fringe" or "pseudo" are not.

But the problem is that there are lots of sciences which have a very hard time coming up with falsifying instances: in particular, the historically-engaged sciences like evolutionary theory, geology, cosmology and so forth. You can't rerun the tape. If someone tells you, *"The universe was created this way,"* and you respond, *"Well, but what's the falsifiable statement?"* it's awfully hard to find one.

HB: It's hard to have another Big Bang.

MG: Exactly. That would be great if we could. But we can't. On the other hand, parapsychology has falsifiable statements everywhere. So does Velikovsky. Velikovsky says, *"If you go get the atmosphere of Venus, it will have hydrocarbons in it."* No one bothers to go. So he makes falsifiable claims all the time, as do creationists, flat-earth people, and many more. Falsifiable claims are everywhere.

HB: What are the "flat-earth falsifiable claims", just out of curiosity?

MG: Well, you can't cross Antarctica straight through, because the earth is flat, with the North Pole in the middle. There are also claims about the bending of light: that sunrise and sunset are optical illusions caused by the fact that light doesn't travel in straight lines. There's a theory, there. It's not a very popular theory, but—

HB: Wow. You have to do a lot of reading in your line of work.

MG: Indeed. Relatedly, one of the things that stands out about Velikovsky is that his prose is really great, and much of the prose in this field is not.

Anyway...the third problem with Popper's criterion is more of a philosophical one: it requires you to not believe in truth. Consistently applying it means that nothing is ever true: scientists make no true claims. I can't say, *"This chair is made of atoms."* I can only say, *"No one has disproved the claim that this chair is made of atoms, yet."* It's a very uncomfortable position to be in long term.

HB: Unless you're Neils Bohr, or somebody like that.

MG: Right. I think most scientists would say, *"I don't think that."* But if you *don't* think that, then falsification hasn't been consistent.

So Popper's bright line of demarcation is very appealing, and it's gotten a lot of press, so people know about it, but it's very problematic.

It's actually the law in the United States now. It's written into a 1982 US District Court decision, McLean vs. Arkansas Board of

Education, which is the decision that says, *"Creation is a religion and not science and therefore can't be in the schools."* William Overton, the judge who made the decision, put in a series of demarcation criteria into the ruling, and one of them is falsifiability.

There's another hearing about intelligent design, a 2005 case called Kitzmiller vs. Dover Area School District. There the judge doesn't use falsifiability, because the testimony at that time says that's actually not a very good criterion. Instead he uses things like "consensus of the scientific community", which is a sociological argument. So now we're back to your earlier point about relativism.

There are features of the scientific world—the scientific theories and the scientific community that we know today—which don't provide bright lines of demarcation but provide you degrees of confidence about what's true and not true.

There are many claims in physics that you might question, but if you question that individual claim, it turns out there are eight claims that would be wrong that are dependent on it, and each of those claims are tied to more things. It's a very consistent system.

Eventually you get to something like the Second Law of Thermodynamics or conservation of energy, you get to something that you're just not going to mess with.

In other words, the whole set of things travel together, and part of the problem many people in the scientific community had with Velikovsky's theories was, *If he's right about this Venus thing, then all these other things we think about orbits don't work. We think those things work for a lot of very good reasons, and those reasons have other good reasons behind them.*

At a certain point there's a lot of inertia.

Science is actually a fairly conservative field this way. People think of it as always revolutionary, always transgressing borders, but there's a lot of built-in agreement with prior knowledge. It's rare that you get a complete transformation and overhaul of everything that people think.

That's one reason for real confidence. Another is that scientists agree about a lot of fundamentals, and there are many points of contact between, say, biology and physics that work well. And that also increases confidence. But, again, you're not going to get a bright line.

Questions for Discussion:

1. Had you heard of Popper's falsifiability criterion before reading this chapter? Has reading this chapter changed your views on its merits or realm of applicability?

2. What does Michael mean, exactly, when he talks about "points of contact" between biology and physics? How is that relevant to the concepts discussed in this chapter?

IX. Fringe Benefits
Seeking a balance

MG: I'm actually quite comfortable with the fact that there's no bright line. I understand why it makes some people antsy, but on the other hand, you also want there to be weird thinking at the edges.

HB: In your book, *The Pseudoscience Wars*, you invoke this idea of a balance: if you're too conservative, if you don't allow *any* heterodox views in whatsoever, then you're not going to have any innovation whatsoever: you're going to have a stagnant field.

MG: Right—you're going to have zero fringe, because anytime someone says something that's not in the orthodoxy, they're out. You can allow a little bit of innovation that way, but very, very little.

HB: So there's this trade-off. And then, of course, if you have too much—if the bar is too low and you let everything in —well, then it's just catastrophic because most of the stuff is just complete nonsense.

MG: And the time budget that you have to expend searching out everything is going to be very hard. I call this the "Central Dilemma".
The point is that somewhere you have to lay that boundary. Let's take a classic example, Einstein's Special Relativity paper of 1905.
It's a crazy paper. It would never have been accepted by peer review. It cites *nothing*. The only experiment it mentions is an experiment a 6-year old can do with a battery and a coil. It seems to refute most of the accepted views of electromagnetism and doesn't deal with many inconsistencies that it seems to raise.

HB: It's beautifully written, though.

MG: It *is* beautifully written. And it's an amazing argument. Now we look at it as canonical, because we also think it's *right*. But the reason why it was accepted at the time is because there was no peer review. The editor in charge of that part of the journal, Max Planck, read it and said, "*This is really interesting. We need to talk about this.*" So he printed it.

That's strongly innovative. Quantum mechanics in all of its forms would *never* have gotten through with a culture of strong peer review. It changes too many of the fundamental assumptions of physics. But editors were willing to let stuff go through, they were willing to experiment, because they thought, "*We're in a bind with some features of atomic physics at the moment and we're willing to relax some of our barriers a bit to get new ideas in.*"

Many of the new ideas are now crazy when you look back at them. Before there was a neutron, for example, people were saying, "*There are only two particles, an electron and a proton, but we seem to have something else that weighs about as much as a proton. It's probably a proton that swallowed an electron, which means that there are electrons in the nucleus of an atom.*" This nuclear-electron theory had about a ten-year lifespan, and then it goes away. Now, of course, if someone told you that there are no neutrons you'd say, "*That's crazy.*" But it's perfectly plausible.

So there are many instances where people are willing to relax how innovative they want to be. Another classic instance of something that's rejected at the time as being too innovative and later comes to be thought of as actually true is continental drift.

When Alfred Wegener first proposes the idea, it's very strongly rejected by American geologists. It's rejected for many reasons, and there's a lot of very good historical scholarship on this.

Much of the argument is along the lines of, "*We don't need this mechanism to explain the continents, and you don't have a mechanism that explains your motion,*" or "*We have better mechanisms that would work in contravention of this; and you can't move through the ocean floors because the ocean floors are actually harder than the continents, so the continents would break apart if they moved across oceans.*"

That's actually true. Our understanding now is that the sea floor spreads and pushes the continents apart. So the theory went into abeyance for about three decades. Wegener dies tragically in Greenland doing experiments in a winter storm; and then in the 1950s his theory starts to become the orthodoxy for how we now think about continents.

The Velikovskians liked this argument. Lots of people in the fringe liked this. They say, *"You see—you guys rejected it and now it's in."* But often things change because new data come in: part of the reason continental drift got accepted in the 1950s is that during the war there was lots of mapping of the ocean floor in the search for Nazi submarines. Suddenly, all these oceanographers are conscripted to do this kind of research, and there is now all this interesting data on bands of strips of magnetic rock on the ocean floor that seems to indicate some kind of sea-floor motion.

In this case, then, had someone been able to decree, *"No one will speak of continental drift again,"* and made it simply vanish without a trace, you'd have to reinvent it later because the new data would compel you to do so.

Letting stuff float on the fringes is a way of getting new ideas and occasionally sharpening one's critical abilities. During the 1970s, when many fringe doctrines are out there, like Erich von Däniken's *Chariots of the Gods* or Velikovsky, many science teachers would assign these books to their science classes, saying, *"The assignment for the midterm is to pick a scientific claim in this book and show why it's wrong."* Then people went out and did research and learned how to make reasoned arguments. That was supposed to be a way of sharpening your teeth.

Questions for Discussion:

1. On the whole, where do you think the scientific community lies on the balance between conservatism and openness? Are there some scientific fields that are more open to whacky, new ideas than others?

2. How would you respond to the claim, "If a scientific theory is true, it will always win out in the end"?

X. Learning From History
Towards better science?

HB: When we consider the importance of raising the public profile of science, triggering the interest of bright, young minds and so forth, it has long seemed to me that there are two separate issues.

The first one concerns teaching people what we currently understand, and the second is teaching people about *the process* of science.

I have the sense that many of the arguments against Velikovsky weren't so much about the particularities of what he was predicting, but the *way* he was going about predicting it: his invocation of nebulous and ill-defined mechanisms, say. You mentioned earlier, in passing, the importance he gives to electromagnetic theory.

MG: Yes. He doesn't believe in gravity.

HB: Well, that's a bit heretical right there.

MG: Yes, indeed.

HB: So it's not just, "*Oh look, Jupiter is, indeed, emitting radio waves and therefore you must absolutely be right, Mr Velikovsky.*" There's an entire logical process of how predictions are being reached at that must be carefully examined.

MG: Right. It's the classic line, *A broken clock is right twice a day*. Just because you've said a true statement among many false statements doesn't mean that we should necessarily believe you. And this very debate does happen in public concerning these theories.

HB: Which brings me to my next point. I could simply say, "*This was an interesting historical situation. There have been others in the past, and there will doubtlessly be others in the future.*"

But what I'd really like to know is how we might, concretely, learn from all of this? Where should we set the bar exactly, between making sure that we're sufficiently innovative but not wasting our time chasing after silly speculations? What should we do in terms of public policy? How should we educate our children about the process of science? How strict should we be in terms of conforming to a set of established beliefs, while recognizing what you said earlier about the causal links to the entire edifice—that it's not just enough to say, '*Well, this could be right, you never know,*' but that we must make explicit the implication that some specific statement might blow up everything we've understood for the past 300 years, which means that we would have to have a parallel justification for everything else we've understood to date—and the likelihood of that being true is extremely small.

I appreciate that it's not your job—you're a historian, you're not the science advisor to the president or anything like that—but is there anything that we can conclude from these past experiences in terms of being more tolerant, less tolerant or whatever?

MG: I have views on these questions, but I'm a historian; and so, as I like to say, the future is none of my business.

HB: OK. But you can put your historian hat away now, because we're just having a conversation.

MG: Yes, we're having a conversation.

So I think this is a central question to ask. I mean, what do we do science education *for*? We do it partially because we want people to know some things, but really we want them to understand something about how we understand what we understand about nature. And I take that extremely seriously.

I think part of my position on this is that, as an outsider to two different fields, I observe something. One is that philosophers have been stuck for a long time trying to figure out sharp demarcation criteria. Many of them now would say, "*Popper's wrong, there are no sharp demarcation criteria, but that doesn't mean that there aren't family resemblances, or certain kinds of things that seem to go together that make science science.*" There's some promise to those particular approaches, but they are fuzzy at the edges, which most philosophers will now tolerate.

Philosophers, then, are struggling with this question. Scientists, on the other hand, don't struggle with it at all.

Every day, every scientist demarcates. They hit delete when they see certain emails, they don't read that paper, they look at some table of contents and say, "*That guy's crazy. I'm not going to look at that.*" They read the abstract, they know it's not worth their time. They say, "*Oh, this one might be worth my time. That guy's crazy too, but sometimes he's right.*" They do this trivially.

To me, instead of feeling despair at the plight of the philosophers, the scientists' interaction with this is actually a source of immense confidence, because we *do* this, we just don't know quite *how* we do it—which means it's a very complex, socially, complicated, embedded process.

HB: And it's not uniform, of course, across fields—

MG: Or personalities. Some geologist might say, "*I'm more willing to tolerate. My bar is lower. I will read more crap in order to get that one interesting idea.*" And somebody else says, "*No, actually I'm pretty set on how mountains are made. I just want to look at the adjustments.*"

Different people, different disciplines, different time periods, different national communities or different educational traditions—say, people educated in Scotland versus Cambridge—would have very different attitudes towards this at different moments.

One thing that historians and sociologists like to do is see what scientists *actually* do. And we can see that it's actually *not* a problem for scientists to do this right now.

So one thing we could do is nothing and just let the system work the way it is. It seems like very few fringe theories that are absolutely empirically wrong have made it, which should give us some sense that this system more or less works.

HB: It may not be maximally efficient, but overall it's pretty effective.

MG: Right. Or we could try to tweak it a bit.

For example, grant-making agencies are one place where this gets manifested. The grants are peer-reviewed, and peer review is a system to set the bar. What ends up happening is that some peer reviewers have a very high bar, some have a very low bar. You could imagine—and this has been proposed for something like long-distance space travel—"*Why don't we do something like the X Prize?*"

We want to figure out how to get a plane that flies into the stratosphere, let's just make it open: let people try whatever crazy theory they want to try and we'll give them a chunk of money at the end. The longitude problem was solved with something similar: "*Let's make it a race and just judge it at the end.*"

Or we could say, "*We have this particular pot of money and we allocate, say, 2% of our budget on R&D to really weird ideas, and just let it go.*"

I was once told anecdotally, so I'm not sure if it's true, that some parapsychology research was funded by McDonnell Douglas or other airplane manufacturers, because if it's possible to manipulate machines with your mind—

HB: The stakes are so high.

MG: Exactly: the stakes are so high, and it's a couple hundred thousand dollars—which is chump change to these guys—so just give it, and see what happens.

Maybe. Maybe we should have some of our money dedicated to the real blue-sky stuff. Maybe psychic stuff actually happens. Wouldn't we like to know? Maybe we should dedicate some of our budget to debunking: certain people could be hired to exclusively go out, find theories, and argue why they're wrong.

Now, what I argue in my Velikovsky book is that I don't think science literacy solves this problem, because the more excited you get people about science—which I think is a wonderful thing, I think it's exactly what we should be doing—the more you're going to get excited people who come up with fringe ideas. As science gets more visible, more people want to be scientists. Since all the fringe people think they're scientists, science literacy generates more of these ideas.

So one thing we could do is to tweak our system to more efficiently explore some of the stuff on the fringes more. We could do nothing. Or we could just relax a little bit about some of this stuff. Most of it has no policy implications, so we can be relaxed about it. Velikovsky's ideas have no policy implications whatsoever. You don't have to worry about them.

Whether we should vaccinate our kids, or allow people not to be vaccinated, has enormous policy implications—more so, I would say, than allowing creationism to be taught in public schools, which obviously has other components associated with it regarding religion and so forth.

The reason why that's even an issue in the US is because education is run here in a decentralized fashion. For countries like France that have a centralized educational system, you could just not include that bit on the exam. It's just not part of "official knowledge" and the problem is solved centrally, easily—

HB: Or, of course, you *could* include it—

MG: Which would take us back to the Soviet genetics problem we spoke about earlier. Clearly there are benefits and weaknesses to both centralization and decentralization.

But at any rate, the large-scale options seem to be that we can tweak it, we can leave it as it is, or we could adopt a more "live and let live" attitude towards some of this stuff and say, "*Look, it doesn't do any harm.*"

Some of it *does* do harm. Eugenics, racial sciences of various kinds, *do* have an enormous negative legacy to deal with. But eugenics wasn't fringe, as it happens, eugenics *was* actually the establishment science. *Criticizing* eugenics was actually fairly fringe in the late 19th century.

Which is all to say that, while history gives you a sense of humility about this, it also tells you that the system we have now is extremely inefficient but seems to be actually getting things done in a way that's more or less satisfactory. Which means, to my mind, that when Congress tries to meddle with the system and says, "*You guys at the National Science Foundation are funding this stuff that's irrelevant,*" I'm not convinced. It seems to me that the system funds some bad stuff and funds some good stuff.

The track record of the system of grant agencies is okay, not great. But the track record for politics meddling with that particular system is very bad. So my thinking is: better not mess with that. It's wishy-washy and hand-wavy, and it doesn't solve the concerns of the anti-relativist man on the street in a necessarily clean way, but it seems to me that that's the way the world works.

Science is one of the most complicated human activities we do. It's global. It's extremely expensive. It's very unintelligible to most people because the barriers to entry are quite high. And the process seems quite wasteful. The median citation rate for a biomedicine article is zero: over half of science biomedical articles that are produced, no one cites. Possibly no one reads. So that's hardly very efficient.

HB: And yet, as a process, on the whole, science is incredibly impactful.

MG: Yes. So we could try to engineer the system to make it more efficient. There were various attempts in the 1930s to do so, but we've been fairly bad at doing that. Some of the innovations have been quite good: the move to the journal, the way online publishing now seems to work, have various benefits to it.

Physicists have basically done away with peer review in the form of the arXiv. Nonetheless, after their article's been out for a while, they still chose to submit it to a journal anyway.

HB: Well, the question of status remains: virtually anyone can get his paper on the arXiv.

MG: Right. Well, anybody who has a .edu email address. There have been demarcation debates about the arXiv as well—there's a thing called "viXra", which is archive backwards: it's an alternative arXiv for stuff that won't get on arXiv: it's got some parapsychology on it (which is what it was started for), but it also has holocaust-denial and other stuff on it.

But, getting back to the larger issue of tweaking the system, I think we could tweak it in ways that would encourage innovation while perhaps leaving ourselves the possibility to sometimes tamp down innovation if we think that there are too many weird theories in some area and we need to really consolidate what we know.

Questions for Discussion:

1. Which of the options discussed in this chapter would you like to see implemented and why?

2. What role do economic factors associated with the publication of academic journals play in these issues?

3. How regularly should government granting agencies be monitored for effectiveness? What criteria should be used? Who should do the monitoring?

4. Is there a danger of scientific activity becoming "too utilitarian" if measured solely in terms of "impact measures"? Has this already happened, to some extent?

XI. Anthropic Digression
Falsifiability today

HB: Just a couple more questions, if I may. Again, I appreciate that your day job is that of a historian, but you're also a keen observer of what is happening now in the scientific world. Do you look at particular issues and debates that are raging in contemporary science and ask yourself about the potential applicability of what you know to these issues?

Let me try to be more specific. As I was reading your book, one thing that popped into my mind that might be relevant to this broader discussion is the so-called anthropic principle in physics. When talking about the anthropic principle, many scientists say things like, *"That's just not science."*

And when they say, *"That's not science,"* they don't mean—or at least don't generally mean—*"You're flaky"* or *"You're the modern-day equivalent of Immanuel Velikovsky,"* they mean that the claims you're making that purport to be scientific are not actually scientific, and here they typically explicitly invoke Karl Popper or slightly watered-down versions of "Popperian" criteria, saying, in effect, *"What you are claiming isn't falsifiable."*

Just to recapitulate the anthropic principle very briefly: there's this idea that there are a huge number of possible paths that the universe might have taken to achieve its present state, but it's recognized that only a very small percentage of them actually will support the conditions that we now find ourselves in (that is, enable atoms to form, support life, what have you).

So the argument goes that, while all of these possible alternatives are in principle equally plausible with no way, a priori, of distinguishing between them, the only thing you can say to answer the question of how it could be that we wound up in the highly specialized circumstances that happen to support our existence is that, had that not been the case, we wouldn't be around to ask the question. In other words, this "choosing of this particular path," in a sense, was already implied by the very fact of our existence long before we sat down to seriously address that very question.

I must admit that I haven't been paying terribly close attention to these matters of late, but some years ago there was a sudden shift in terms of a particular type of physicist who was invoking this kind of reasoning. Many who, a few years before were responding with scorn and derision to those explicitly referencing the anthropic principle—claiming that it was nothing more than an "unfalsifiable cop out"—suddenly started using it themselves.

So this is a long preamble to the following question: Do you see any direct parallels with these previous questions of demarcation and the like that we were talking about earlier and the anthropic principle, or anything else in science? And do you feel that people are treating these concepts (demarcation, falsifiability, verificationism) with the appropriate amount of sophistication?

MG: Hmm. That's a great question. The way I would start to think about this is that there's a lot of rather interesting blurring (we would call it blurring, looking on the outside of science and philosophy) that always happens.

The reason why I say we would call it "blurring from the outside", is because on the inside, much of science is philosophical already. For example, atomism used to be an ethical precept in antiquity. Part of the point about atoms and the void was an argument against the gods, that everything has a randomness built into it, the world isn't deterministic.

When you read Lucretius' *On the Nature of Things*, the first two books are about the physical world, and most of the rest of it is about how we should behave towards other people. It's as if you needed the atomists to get the ethical precepts, but the point is the ethics. There's always been blurring like that.

What triggers my attention most is when you start to get a fight. For me, that's one of the lessons from the Velikovsky story: that there are certain flashpoint moments when people argue about pseudo-science more than other times.

There's a flashpoint around the same time that Darwin's views come out in the 1860s (*The Origin of Species* is published in 1859), which is also the time when spiritualism, séances and the existence of ghosts is actively discussed.

There's a flashpoint in the late 1940s and early 1950s; and there seems to be a flashpoint right about now, with vaccines, global warming and a whole bunch of effects.

Those flashpoints, I think, have historical and political moments that we can associate with them. There's a change in the stability of the institutions that we're used to, dramatic transformations in the status of science—up or down (right now, for physics, it's down: once the dominant science, physics is now ceding much of its cultural authority to biomedicine and molecular biology), the rise of patents as a way of funding science, and so forth.

The science system has been undergoing enormous transformation since the 1970s, which is a very interesting thing to look at, but it has these consequences. One of the things that happens when you lose some of your visibility is that you're able to allow more risks in, and the anthropic principle seems to me precisely that: it's being entertained now, at a moment when people say, "*You know, the fine-tuning problem, this problem about the constants, is actually an interesting problem. Let's try to think through ways of meaningfully addressing it. And if we're going to think that through, we have to drop the bar: we have to actually allow some weirder ideas in and see whether they might work.*"

Whereas, back when you were trying to make detailed measurements of the cosmic microwave background radiation, you had more than enough stuff to do: you're busy, it's expensive, you have grant lines and so on.

Similarly, you start to see much more speculation about the fundamentals of quantum physics in the 1970s when there's a massive crash in the job market. This is something a colleague of mine at MIT, David Kaiser, has worked on extensively: there's a big hiring boom from the 1950s and 1960s, and then a recession happens in the 1970s that frees people up to do different kinds of things, because you're unemployed or partially employed and you no longer have to churn out grants because there aren't any.

HB: You can do what you want to do.

MG: Right. You can do what you want to do. And when you do that, you allow certain levels of expansion. To me, the rise of the anthropic principle as a plausible idea, the rise of the multiverse as a plausible idea, those are interesting markers of something that's happening within the physical sciences.

I don't know whether we should or shouldn't entertain these ideas, but the point is that people are. These ideas have been around for a long time, but when do they suddenly start to get legs? That usually tells you something about how the community is thinking about restructuring itself.

For some people in the community, that's naturally very nerve-wracking, but for me the fact that this is now being entertained is a very exciting moment.

As you know, for the anthropic principle, there's a strong and a weak form. The weak form is basically an epistemological claim that says that we can only speak about what we can observe; and we can observe *this*.

The strong form—that the world has somehow evolved to evolve us—I understand why people are uncomfortable with it. But often when you get discomfort, it's because people aren't necessarily talking about the same thing: some people are advocating one thing, while others are advocating another.

That's a normal situation in the sciences. The real fights about string theory seem to me to have happened in the 1990s and the early 2000s, when there was a very active charge of, "*This isn't science. This is pseudoscience. There's no connection to experiment. It's not real.*"

That seems to me, as an outsider, less visible now. To me, that says that the community has stopped being worried about a particular set of issues and is now worried about something else.

Questions for Discussion:

1. To what extent do prevailing social and economic factors influence the sort of science that people do? Would Einstein have become a biologist had he been born a century later?

2. How do you think the Covid-19 pandemic of 2020 will impact future scientific research and discovery?

XII. Better Science?
Educated by history

HB: It seems to me that you are astutely paying attention to what is going on in the present-day scientific community.

MG: As much as I can.

HB: But are scientists paying attention to you and your colleagues? Are they paying attention to historians of science, sociologists of science, philosophers of science?

After all, you've looked long and hard at how scientific ideas evolve, how they gain currency or don't gain currency, what some of the factors might be. This seems like something a practicing scientist might well be directly interested in.

Is that true? In your experience, are practicing scientists interested in and influenced by historical arguments, not just because they think they're intellectually interesting, but because they actually believe that getting a deeper appreciation of history and sociology of science might actually be relevant to them in their day job?

MG: It's a great question. The field of the history of science grew out of scientists who then started doing historical work; and it was hand-in-glove, the two fields were seen as belonging together.

Often historians of science were in physics departments. They would teach introductory physics and they would talk to their colleagues.

I would say that there are probably about three possible positions, and different fields have them in different ways.

First, there are people who think it's absolutely irrelevant—or if not irrelevant, just nice stories. It's fun to know Einstein anecdotes, for example: *"Please tell me that the Einstein anecdotes I know are true; and if they're not, tell me some new ones that are true that I might use."* Among chemists, you see a lot of interest in the history of science, but a lot of that interest is as a kind of entertainment. They're interested in the past of their field because they're chemists and they like chemistry, and they want to know what these great geniuses did and how we came to know what we know. That's great. I think that's a wonderful way of thinking about it. I'm not so crazy about people who reject the correct stories in favour of the "better stories". Sometimes the "better stories" are true and sometimes they're not.

HB: But if all you're interested in is storytelling, I suppose it doesn't make any difference.

MG: I suppose it doesn't make any difference, but it makes a difference to me, because I feel that there's truth and untruth about what actually happened.

Physicians are also very often interested in the past of their field. There's a lot of interest in the history of medicine. Anyway, that's one position.

There's a second position, which is the other extreme: people who think it's threatening. This was sometimes the case with physicists, most prominently in the 1990s, when historians of science were felt by some to somehow undercut the status of science, making it look less pristine, less true, less pure.

By focusing on things like eugenics and the dirty underbelly of some of the sciences, or these fringe theories, or things like fraud, or when scientists behave not according to the norms they're supposed to behave by, it makes science look bad and it gives aid and comfort to the enemies of science.

That's not a very constructive point of view. I think most historians, sociologists and philosophers of science study science because they *like* science. That's why they do it. They're fascinated by it. I am. I want to know more about how it actually works. It's one of the most important forces in the world today: I would like to know how it operates. It's a human activity done by humans. It therefore has flaws and warts and so on, but I can understand why in certain positions some people might find that insulting, even though that's not at all the intention of the field. Yet that's another position people have, and I think at certain moments that's very prominent.

The third position—which is, I think, a minority view in the physical sciences, but is often true among biologists—is what you point to, which is: *we could learn something about science by studying its history. We could learn about theories that have been abandoned but maybe should be resurrected, or certain phenomena that people used to investigate but now don't.*

There's a philosopher of science at University of Cambridge called Hasok Chang, who did some research on temperature. *How do we know that water boils at 100 degrees, given that we didn't have thermometers that worked until we could calibrate them at 100 degrees?* It turns out that water can boil at a very wide range of temperatures. Depending on whether the container is made of glass or metal, whether you shook the water in advance or not, you can make water boil at 110 degrees, 115 degrees, or what have you.

People used to investigate this question, and then they stopped. Maybe there's some physics there that we could learn if we went back and actually asked those questions again. Historians can bring up old, unresolved questions and put them in front of scientists.

Or historians can say something like, "*Justus von Liebig ran a really good laboratory and trained lots of students. If you want to found an institute or found a school, here's what successful people have done in the past, here's what failures have happened in the past. They may not work for you in the future, but you can learn ideas from them.*"

Biologists, especially evolutionary biologists, are very interested in some of the debates that philosophers or historians of biology have about Darwin, Wallace, and early strands of evolutionary theory that petered out or were refuted. There are active debates going back to the original sources that help shed light on—if not the right answer—at least different approaches to the right answer.

The sentiment here is, "*Darwin was a very smart guy and he thought about a lot of these things, so maybe we should go back and look and perhaps excavate those things.*"

There's a smaller set of people who want to learn from the history of science and think it can teach us something about how we could or should organize science.

The Soviet Union had a very different way of organizing science than the US did. The system in the former Soviet Union is now undergoing a transformation to look much more like the American system. Globally, too, that's been true: the Europeans used to have very different ways of organizing science in terms of grants, tenure and so forth and now, everything is moving towards an American model.

The American model seems to be good, but it's not the only model, and there might well be a risk of monoculturing, of having just one way of doing things. The history of science enables you to hold up things from the past and say, "*Look at that. This was another way of doing it. It had costs and it had benefits. Before you reject it, look at those costs and benefits.*"

You may decide at the end of the day that the system we have now is a good one, but the act of developing this broader perspective is a function that the history of science can serve, and often does serve. The people who get more interested in the history of science seem to be older scientists: perhaps they're not doing as much active work anymore and their stuff is now historical so that more historians come talk to them. They also tend to be people with a greater voice in science policy.

And one way in which the history of science comes to do something for science policy is when scientists look back and say, "*Well, actually, when we allowed for patents to be given to universities for publicly-funded research, that had **these** consequences. We can try to ameliorate those consequences or not care about them, but we should see that the sociologists have documented that.*"

I think that's one of the reasons why it's important that a community of people like me is out there, just trying to figure out as much as we can about this enterprise, because science is not going to go away. It does have enormous consequences; and we would like to know how it operates and possibly improve it and improve our lives in general. It's possible that history has lessons that let people do that. The historians don't go about prescribing those histories, but we do try to provide the material for those who want to.

HB: That's a wonderful point to end on. Do you have anything else that you'd like to add?

MG: I don't think so. We got to Popper; we talked about relativism, which I wasn't sure we were going to get to. No, I think that's it.

HB: Well, I had a great time. Thank you very much, Michael. That was a lot of fun.

MG: Thank you. It *was* a lot of fun.

Questions for Discussion:

1. Should all scientists be exposed to a course or two of the history of science as part of their education?

2. To what extent does globalization increase the likelihood of "monoculturing" the structures of scientific organization, and possibly the resulting science itself?

Continuing the Conversation

Readers are encouraged to read Michael's book, *The Pseudoscience Wars: Immanuel Velikovsky and the Birth of the Modern Fringe*, which goes into considerable additional detail about many issues discussed here, as well as his more 2021 book, *On the Fringe: Where Science Meets Pseudoscience*. Michael is a prolific and engaging author who has written on a number of other topics ranging from the history of the Periodic Table (*A Well-Ordered Thing: Dmitrii Mendeleev and the Shadow of the Periodic Table*), Einstein (*Einstein in Bohemia*), the impact of language on science (*Scientific Babel: How Science Was Done Before and After Global English*), the history of America's use of nuclear weapons at the end of WWII (*Five Days in August: How World War II Became a Nuclear War*) and many more.

The Consolations of History

A conversation with Teofilo Ruiz

Introduction
In the Marrow

Teofilo Ruiz is a teacher.

Notwithstanding all the trappings of academic success—the PhD from Princeton, the prestigious fellowships, the National Humanities Medal, membership in the American Academy of Arts and Sciences—that is, quite simply, how Teo regards himself.

The outside world might well view him as a highly-regarded professional historian who has written numerous scholarly articles and books on a wide variety of social and cultural practices of late medieval and early modern Spain.

But when you talk to Teo, it is always the teacher who comes to the fore. And it was that way, it seems, from the very beginning, instilled in him from his boyhood days in Cuba.

> "*I wanted to teach: that's what I wanted to do. I come from a family of teachers. All my aunts, nine of them, were teachers. I never thought of becoming a scholar or writing books or anything like that: I wanted to be a teacher. I took a history major, but it could have been a philosophy major—I had that as a minor.*
>
> "*When people ask me, 'What do you do?' I never tell them that I write books. I tell them that I'm a teacher—that is what I love to do. I'm coming to the end of it now, but I still love it.*"

Why? What is it about teaching that Teo finds so captivating?

Part of it is clearly the performance itself, the ability to captivate and intrigue. When reminiscing about one of his mentors, the famed

Princeton cultural historian Carl Schorske, Teo seemed immediately transported back to graduate school.

> *"Carl Schorske is the best teacher I have ever seen in my life. He was incredibly keen on teaching undergraduates. It was a performance: he had music behind him and images. It was so elegant and beautiful that you were utterly seduced by it."*

Teo, too, freely admits that he loves to perform in front of a classroom, that the experience itself impassions and inspires him to rhetorical heights. But it is more than just entertainment, of course. At its heart, teaching is about communicating values.

> *"I always say to them, 'Don't think of yourself as the final product of an evolutionary and historical process that culminates with you.*
>
> *'These people living in the first or fifth century in India or China, or in the 12th or 16th century in France or Spain, were facing issues not so different from the ones that you may be facing. Here is how they tried to get through their lives and their difficult periods.*
>
> *'Their answers are not always right. They may have consequences that lead to awful things. But these are people who are alive.'"*

Are alive? I remember thinking to myself. *The present tense? A slip of the tongue?* Not at all, as it turned out.

> *"This is something that I said too in The Terror of History. I want to convey to my students the fact that many of these people who wrote, or who lived, or who were peasants in a village—which I had tried to at least name, to bring them back to life—are as alive as many of us, because they live on in our memory and our consciousness, because we read them, because we are moved by the way they wrote, because we adore the music they wrote or the paintings they made.*
>
> *"These are not cultural products that you somehow own, these are cultural products that serve as a link to all humans who lived before you. You must understand that these wonderful, cultural trophies, as Walter Benjamin once said, are always paid with a terrible, terrible price.*

> *"Take The Industrial Revolution: this unique moment in which places like England and the Netherlands, then Germany and France—catapult into great, global dominance, a dominance that is paid for by their workers in those satanic mills that Blake described so vividly..."*

An important message, to be sure. But are we learning? Are we remembering? Are the diligent efforts of Teo and his like-minded colleagues bearing fruit?

There are definitely moments when Teo himself seems to have lost hope.

> *"I am actually not unhappy to be the age that I am. I love my undergraduates. I teach because I also love the students: there is something that happens in the classroom—not always, but sometimes—there is a moment of recognition, the moment when a life is transformed.*
>
> *"But I am glad that I am the age that I am, when the end is near, both of my teaching and of my life, because I think that for the first time we are teaching a generation that has completely grown up in a technologically-shaped world.*
>
> *"It's not that they don't know anything or that they are stupid. But they don't know the things I know, they don't have the same frames of reference that I have, they don't really share a common culture with me.*
>
> *"They know other things that I do not know. Am I being antiquarian? Am I being an ultra-reactionary who still thinks that there is value to knowing poetry or knowing history?"*

Behold the jaded and despondent professor, the genteel, old-fashioned communicator who fears he can no longer deeply connect with today's undergraduates.

But then, suddenly, the old teacher bounces back, chattering excitedly about next week's lecture to seventh-grade teachers on medieval history as part of the innovative California History-Social Science Project, or his rewarding interaction with the young-adult writer Avi.

"He saw one of my recorded lectures, and got the idea of writing a novel about an English boy in 1381 during the peasant uprising. And he wrote to me and said that he was writing this young-adult fiction book and asked if I would like to take a look at the final product.

"He sent it to me and it was pretty accurate. I made some tiny fixes here and there, and he ended up dedicating the book to me. It's called Crispin: The Cross of Lead and it won the 2003 Newbery Medal for children's literature. So that's something that I'm very proud of."

There is no quit in Teacher Teo.

The Conversation

I. The Terror of History

The story of a book

HB: I picked up this book called *The Terror of History* not too long ago. It begins with a portrayal of 14th-century Florence during the bubonic plague amongst all the death and dying. We begin with *The Decameron* by Giovanni Boccaccio, where he discusses how people react to the utter catastrophe that has befallen them.

As Boccaccio tells the tale, people respond to this overwhelming crisis in three different ways: there are those who turn to religion, those who begin to live exclusively for the moment—indulging in drinking, fornicating and generally having as good a time as possible—and those who leave, and might later, like Boccaccio, write books. To this outline, you add a fourth category: those who stay and tend the sick and the weak, those who struggle through the darkness and the despair all around them at great personal risk to themselves.

So this is the way your tale begins. And I think to myself, *"That is what this book, The Terror of History, is all about: it's a historical account of how we respond to the terrors and traumas that have consistently befallen us throughout history."*

I've got my finger on it now. I've figured it out. And since it's written by a historian, I'm expecting a cool, objective account of things, perhaps with some grand thesis linking different cataclysmic events thrown in for good measure.

But then the book starts to change. The author mixes in personal reminiscences. Questions arise of a more metaphysical and philosophical nature: *How can we ascribe meaning to existence? How can we pursue the good life amid so much pain and struggle? What can we learn from history? Can we change for the better?*

At the beginning, this was pretty off-putting, because I wasn't expecting it and wasn't at all sure how to react. I generally like to have a clear sense of what a book's about when I start: what the author's angle is, what he or she is trying to tell me.

But then I began to loosen up and enjoy the experience, seizing the opportunity to more personally engage with you rather than simply read a standard book on history. Is that the sort of effect you were striving for?

TR: This book had a very long genesis. It's really a bit of a narcissistic endeavour, because while I am concerned with the world at large and how people react to catastrophes (like Florence under the plague, but other cases as well), to a large extent, it's also about me. I can tell you something about how it got finished. For over 40 years, I've taught a class on mysticism, religion and witchcraft, which I named "The Terror of History" because, essentially, it is a way in which people react to these catastrophes.

It dealt mostly with religion, both orthodox and heterodox. I made a recording of this course for *The Teaching Company*; and there had long been the possibility of also publishing it as a book, because that way it could also be a sort of manual that could be used in my classes.

But as I was doing this, a very perceptive reader said, *"No, this is something different. It's about you. It's about what you want to do."* So I began to write this thing with no intention whatsoever of publishing it. I really did it for myself. In that sense, then, there really is that element of faux-memoir: it's not a memoir, it's not an autobiography, it's more about letting out little pieces of myself.

That is something that I began doing in a very difficult period in my life when I was having serious issues with my personal life. I began to write little stories, one per year. These were not intended for publication: they were little anecdotes, little stories. Sometimes I couldn't write directly about what was bothering me. When my father died, I couldn't write about that, so I wrote something else instead, something comic: describing what happens to Cubans when they go to the airport.

HB: What happens to Cubans when they go to the airport?

TR: Well, Cubans love airports. Everybody goes to welcome you when you arrive: there are at least 20 people at the airport waiting for each incoming passenger, while everyone looks around them wondering who is arriving. It's always like that. If you say to a Cuban that you're going to the airport, he'll reply, "*Oh, you're going to the airport? I'll come with you, why not?*"

HB: You too?

TR: Absolutely. It's inconceivable for someone to arrive and for me to not be there waiting. It's a cultural thing, a kind of, shall we say, cultural vestige that remains.

Anyway, I began writing these pieces for *The Terror of History* in much the same fashion as these stories that I used to write. Then I began, more or less, to connect them. And the book lingered on. Frankly, I thought that it was such a self-indulgent book that I didn't ever want to publish it, but Brigitta van Rheinberg at Princeton University Press actually liked it a lot. I also had a scholarly book coming out on festivals and kings' travels in the 16th century at the time (*A King Travels: Festive Traditions in Late Medieval and Early Modern Spain*), for which the great Spanish historian John Elliott was one of the readers, and somehow it became a reasonable thing to publish them both at the same time. So that's how the book came out.

My favourite part of the book is actually the last chapter about aesthetics, this understanding of the world through aesthetics, through a search for beauty or knowledge. I wrote that in Paris, and one of the things that emerges at that point is the deep awareness of being in Paris and reading Proust and connecting all of that.

At any rate, the book is two books: one about me—disguised in many ways, presented in a kind of very hesitant and restricted fashion—and another one about historical processes.

The point here is not an original one, it's one inspired by Walter Benjamin and other people: that the world as it exists is a particularly painful place to be; and we try to make meaning of it in many different ways.

It's not even a question of facing a tragedy or facing a catastrophe, it's simply, *"What do we do? How do we come to terms with the lives we live? What do we do that gives meaning to our lives, when deep inside we know that there is no meaning?"*

HB: Because this searching for meaning is a fundamental aspect of the human condition: it would happen whether or not our society is being ravaged by the bubonic plague.

TR: Right. If there is not one thing, there is another.

HB: Your self-deprecating nature, your lack of bombast, is definitely something that comes across in print as well as in person. You used the word "narcissistic" a few moments ago, and you seem almost compelled to point out that what you are saying is not always original. But I can say that as a reader, it's enjoyable to see you forthrightly air your views. I hope you will continue to do so throughout this discussion.

TR: Well, I always have difficulties doing that. I don't think it's so much a sense of modesty, but more a deep understanding that I can't pontificate, I can't pretend to really know more than I truly know. And what I do know is that there is always this knowing doubt, this sense that I am sort of faking my way through life. I really mean that, this is not for the purpose of this conversation.

This is a sense that I had very strongly as an adolescent: that a part of me was somehow looking on, while the other part of me was acting. I have that deep sense of division within myself. There is a very critical, cynical part of me that looks hard at the way I live my life and the things I do, the things I write. I am always hesitant to pontificate or argue or hold views with total and complete conviction.

I've been strongly influenced by books I read during my formative years, and I always remember Nietzsche saying that it's not a question of having the strength of your convictions or your ideals, but rather questioning those ideals and those convictions all the time.

Now, I have views that are very solid, politically. I'm very much on the left, for example. But then I also realize that, while it's very lovely to espouse views in public, or to my students, about the injustices and inequalities of the world, I am complicit in this inequality too.

HB: Sure, but that shouldn't prevent you from espousing your views regardless.

TR: I know. But there is an extra step that I should take, which I obviously have not taken, another road that I did not follow, which would have been a more difficult road but perhaps one closer to the kinds of things that I think a human being should be doing.

HB: This all sounds very Catholic to me: all this guilt that you're directing at yourself. Perhaps that's a good segue to your youth, because I think there's a fascinating story there that also blends in well with a broader historical period, which seems to be a developing theme of this conversation. So tell me more about your youth and your Catholic upbringing that seemed to have such a decided effect on your psyche.

TR: Yes. I call it the Buñuel Syndrome, after Luis Buñuel, the famous filmmaker who made films like *Belle de Jour*. He is, of course, anti-clerical and an atheist, but he could not help making films about religion all the time. This is what I call "The Buñuel Effect": you don't like it, you are against it, but you cannot get away from it—you are born and brought up in this "web of significance", as Clifford Geertz would put it.

Questions for Discussion:

1. Do you think historians are, on the whole, better-placed or worse-placed to write memoirs given their professional experiences and orientations?

2. What do you suppose Teo is alluding to when he speaks of "another road that I did not follow"?

II. Becoming a Historian
From Cuba to City College to NYU to Princeton

TR: I grew up in Cuba from a Spanish, Castilian, family, so we were kind of outsiders in our society because we still had ties to Spain: my family went back and forth between Spain and Cuba. I grew up across the street from Hemingway.

HB: Really?

TR: Yes. I could show you a dedication he gave me from *The Old Man and the Sea*.

I spent a great deal of my youth lying on top of a stone table which was on the very edge of Hemingway's farm next to the farm of another American named Frank Steinhart Jr., who was the man who owned the trolleys in Cuba in the 1940s and 1950s. I didn't understand who Hemingway was, exactly, but I was part of a kind of large retinue.

HB: But you knew that he wrote books, presumably?

TR: Yes, I did. I knew he had written *The Old Man and the Sea*; and the truth of the matter was that I did not like his writing at all. I found it very sparse.

HB: Well, it is. It is very sparse.

TR: Of course, I read it in a Spanish translation.

HB: It's sparse in English too.

TR: In fact, I used one of his books in my class in Paris, which is *A Moveable Feast*, because that is a book I really like.

HB: Well, that's a different sort of book, of course.

TR: Yes. It's a memoir, an evocation of being in Paris in the 1920s. At any rate, what I was reading when I was younger were really French romances, as well as Walter Scott in translation, which is a very different way of seeing the world. So I was very much taken by that, but also by the fact that, as strange as it may seem, I went to a Catholic high school and grew up with a kind of radical interpretation of the world that was really nurtured by reading people like St. Francis of Assisi.

Then the revolution came in 1959 when I was 16 years old. And the revolution was another form of religion.

Of course the Catholic Church has been extremely reactionary, but Catholic thought on questions of property and poverty and the like can also be very radical, like St. Francis or the new Pope (also named Francis, as it happens), or in the aspects of the Gospel that richness is a form of sinfulness and the rich man will not be admitted into heaven.

But the revolution in that first glorious year, where one felt very enormous and large, was a very significant and important transformation in my life. I have a very ambivalent attitude towards the Cuban Revolution and to what it became. But it is always ambivalent. It has never been partisan one way or the other. I did not go back to Cuba for 51 years, until I went back two years ago.

HB: I'd love to hear more about that, but let's go first back. So, you're 16, the revolution breaks out...

TR: Yes. I had been active in some anti-Batista movements in my town, something very minor, carrying pamphlets here and there, painting walls.

HB: What was your parents' reaction to all of this?

TR: My parents were very much against Batista, so they were completely for it.

HB: So there was no rebellion against your parents or anything?

TR: No. I had, strangely enough, an extraordinarily spoiled life as I was growing up. My father was a very erudite human being. He was a lawyer.

HB: An erudite lawyer? That seems pretty unusual. Perhaps not in Cuba, though...

TR: Well, in Latin America things are different. Doctors and lawyers read other things there. He actually hated the law. He was a terrible lawyer because he had no interest in it. He read widely on things that were part and parcel of Latin American culture in the 1950s that did not look to Spain at all—because of course, this was during the Franco years—but looked naturally to France or Germany.

He was very fond of Goethe. For my part, I was reading Hermann Hesse before I came to America. Before Hesse became a kind of idol of the 1960s, I was reading *Siddhartha*, *The Journey to the East* and *The Glass Bead Game*, in Cuba, in Spanish. My father was also very interested in the French poets of the 19th century, Verlaine and so forth, so I picked this up too.

It was not that he was so unique in that; he was part of a shared culture. One of the things that I remember very fondly is that he did not work every day of the week. The family also had property and a factory that made preserves from tropical fruits, and I would often accompany him when he went to Havana, where there would be a literary gathering of writers, including one of the best Cuban writers ever, José Lezama Lima.

I remember sitting there waiting for the latest works from Paris—Camus had a tremendous impact on my youth. I read *The Rebel* or *The Myth of Sisyphus* while I was in my late teens, and was not only influenced by that, but also by Camus' own life and commitments.

HB: So you come from this privileged, cultured, intellectually-dynamic background, and then the revolution hits. Then what happens?

TR: Then what happened was, for reasons that were not ideological, a friend was killed in a bar over a prostitute by a member of the Rebel Army. And the killer was not brought to trial. As a result, a group of us sort of resigned from the revolution, which is something that you do not do. You can't resign from revolutions: you are either for them or against them.

I became involved with a group that had been part of a revolution—in fact, the leader was somebody who had been a minister in the first Castro government, Manuel Ray. So I became more involved and ended up imprisoned around the time of The Bay of Pigs.

What happened was that shortly before the invasion, there was a large act of sabotage in Havana, the main department store in Havana—which was called El Encanto, and today is a park—was burned to the ground.

Those who did this were engaged in—I should call it what it really was—anti-revolutionary activities. Even though we really thought of ourselves as the true revolutionaries, we were not, really.

I knew about this event. I had no part in it; and we didn't know about The Bay of Pigs, which was essentially a CIA coup that caught people by complete surprise and which actually wrecked the resistance to the Castro regime that came from the left. It's a very complicated story. But the Cuban government was incredibly active in eliminating from the street anyone that they thought could lead to trouble.

By the 17th of April when the attack occurred, I was already in prison, but because of the policy of preventative incarceration there were over 100,000 people in the prisons. This was a world before computers: they didn't know who was there and they began to release people slowly. I came out with hepatitis, which I contracted from eating spoiled food. And then I was taken again for two days for questioning. At that point it was clear to me that the time to leave Cuba had arrived.

HB: How did you leave Cuba?

TR: The government let people out from time to time.

HB: So you didn't have to do anything heroic?

TR: No. I went to the Brazilian embassy to get political asylum. Then I came to Florida. I was first detained in Miami and sent to Opa-locka, an air force base, because somebody had accused me of being a communist. I spent a few days in a detention center in Opa-locka.

HB: So you had the chance to sample different detention centers of two different regimes, as it were.

TR: Yes. I hated Miami, because it was crawling with Batista followers, the old guard from the Batista days, for whom all the rest of us, like me, were just communists who should have stayed in Cuba. I arrived in October 1961, and I got a job painting in a hotel, the Hotel Casablanca on 66th and Collins Ave. It was 7 days a week, 90 cents an hour. If you missed one day you were out. That lasted 21 days. Then I worked in a sort of a sugar mill in the center of the state.

By then I realized that this was absolutely no life for me, and a very adventurous young woman, a cousin of a cousin of mine, decided that she wanted to drive to New York and I went with her. In March of 1962 we arrived in New York with no money.

I'll always remember, it was the 15th of March when we arrived in New York, and the city was magical, filled with people. We slept in the subway the first night because we didn't have a place to stay.

The next day I went over to someone I had never met before, a relative of one of my relatives, and said to him, "*We are here, my cousin and I; we need a place to stay and we need to do work.*" So he lent us some money and we rented a little room in a house on 138th and Broadway and I began to work on the second floor of a Woolworth's cafeteria right across from Macy's. I started out as a dishwasher and then became a busboy.

HB: You must not have had any English when you first arrived.

TR: I thought I did. In school back in Cuba, I had studied some English, although I had taken more French. But when I arrived in the States, I couldn't understand a word. I couldn't communicate. Later I realized why: when my teacher arrived in New York, I went to pick him up and I had to translate for him.

I worked in Woolworth's for a time, and then I moved to Continental Can Company, a factory that made cans. It was a very good job. Those were the days when blue-collar workers made very good salaries. The people who worked there were mostly Hungarian refugees from 1956. They were trained, highly-skilled labourers. They all had houses in Long Island and two cars. It was a very different world.

Then, in 1962, I went into the army. It was before the Missile Crisis. I was active with Cuban groups and wanted to go back to Cuba; and we were told, very clearly, that there was a unit that was being organized within the US army for a possible invasion of Cuba.

So, on October 12th, 1962, Columbus Day, a recruiting office opened on 53rd and Lexington. I went there, then I went downtown to Manhattan where there was an army station, and we were flown to Fort Knox the following day.

The first unit was 250 Cubans, which eventually grew to 5,000, and we were to be landed in Cuba.

HB: This was a sort of Bay of Pigs II?

TR: It was during the Missile Crisis. The idea was to give them legitimacy. They were going to land this group of Cubans who were going to declare themselves a "republic in arms" to allow the Americans to intervene. Somebody should really write about this: I have all the documentation upstairs.

After they eventually established the agreement by which Khrushchev pulled out the missiles from Cuba in return for which the American government guaranteed the survival of Castro, we were told, *"That's it, we are not going in."*

We would have all been killed: we were canon fodder. These are the kinds of things that only young people can do when they are stupid enough. At any rate, I spent six months in the army.

HB: What was your citizenship status at that time? How did that work when you first came from Cuba?

TR: I essentially came to the United States as an illegal immigrant and became a parolee: I was paroled from the United States since I did not have a visa to enter the country. The American government extended conditions to the Cubans, which I find very unjust, in that Cubans who arrive in the United States were all given a special parolee status for political reasons.

HB: That part of American government policy I know. But then how were you somehow allowed to go into the army?

TR: Well, I should show you the documentation of all this. Our dog tags and our registration numbers were different from the US ones. Theirs was designated as RA (regular army), while ours was UC. It was very clear that we were going to be sent in as a kind of vanguard and be followed, which was the idea of The Bay of Pigs except that—

HB: It didn't work.

TR: Well, the President did not know this. I actually know a great deal about that because my professor at Princeton (whom I truly love, one of my academic fathers), was, in the old tradition, somebody who consulted for foreign policy.

According to him, and he was at the Oval Office when The Bay of Pigs went down, Kennedy was very undecided about what to do. Adlai Stevenson was the one who said, *"No, you can't go in. It will ruin you if you do this."* And he pulled out.

In any case, I came out of the army in April of 1963 and went back to my job. I became active in kind of counter-revolutionary activity, training myself to be infiltrated into Cuba.

I began seeing somebody who was the daughter of a well-to-do family near my hometown, and I said to myself, "*Well, if I am not in Cuba by May 20th 1964, we will marry.*"

Then the man who was the leader of the group that I was part of was caught in the Bahamas gambling the money away that we had collected, so that was the end of my revolutionary years.

I got married and went back to school, to City College of New York, while still working in the factory.

HB: So why did you decide to go to City College? Did you think to yourself, *I'm frustrated, I want a life of the mind now*? Or was it something else? How did that come about?

TR: Well, I had expectations, intellectual expectations. The factory work was very good: I could read while I worked. But I wanted to go and learn. Life at the factory was fun. It was the beginning of the Vietnam years and we did "guerilla theatre" in the bathroom during the smoke breaks. We listened to Bob Dylan, and it was great.

I had gone to City College when I arrived in New York to take English as a Second Language, but at the time I was not ready, emotionally or otherwise, to attend full-time, so I quit.

I got married in June of 1964 and went back to school the following September. I did fairly well, mostly because I had received a very substantial education during my years in Cuba.

HB: Were you studying Spanish history then, or history in general, or something else entirely?

TR: You see, I always talk about serendipity. I wanted to teach: that's what I wanted to do. I come from a family of teachers. All my aunts, nine of them, were teachers. I never thought of becoming a scholar or writing books or anything like that: I wanted to be a teacher. I took a history major, but it could have been a philosophy major—I had that as a minor.

HB: It was a means to an end to become a teacher.

TR: Yes. But there was a natural focus in the humanities: I clearly was not very good at math or anything like that. Like many other people, I had been enchanted by the Middle Ages after reading a textbook by Joseph R. Strayer, so that's what I was going to do.

HB: This was the gentleman who became your supervisor at Princeton, right?

TR: That is correct.

HB: Was this also the fellow who was advising Kennedy? Is this the same guy? Am I following the story correctly? What's a medievalist doing advising Kennedy?

TR: Yes, that is correct. Joseph Strayer was a member of the famous Princeton class of 1925/1926 when the Dulles brothers were at Princeton, Allen and John Foster Dulles. In 1939, they organized the OSS, the precursor to the CIA, and during WW II they drew upon scholars from that Princeton group as consultants.

Then when it became the CIA, which Allen Dulles ran for many years, there was this natural Princeton connection. Every year at class reunions, all of these operatives met to discuss and come to Washington to provide advice. In the 1970s and 1980s we all disliked this immensely and fought against it because it was a kind of meretricious service to the government. But in retrospect those were very innocent years, because I think that this country could have benefited more recently from having some historians tell the President, "*Don't get into this place, you're going to get in a lot of trouble here.*"

At any rate, I went to City College and did very well. I continued working throughout: I worked during the day and went to school in the evening. To me, it remains one of those golden ideals. At the time, it was free: City College was free. And it was an incredibly nurturing environment. Most of my teachers were German refugees and the classes were very small. It was a tremendous experience, very positive; and I was caught up in it.

I went and talked to someone who taught there part-time, but who was also the head of the Social Science department at Washington Irvine High School in Union Square. I told him, "*I want to teach primary or secondary school.*"

He turned to me and said, "*With that accent? Impossible. You should go and get a degree and teach in college where it doesn't really matter.*" So that's how I ended up applying to graduate school. I applied to Princeton, but didn't get in. So I went to NYU for an MA, and then re-applied to Princeton after that and got in.

When I entered NYU, which was a more demanding program than the BA at City College, I quit my job at the factory and became both a superintendent in a building in Astoria, Queens, and a cab driver, four times a week. I drove a cab in New York from 1969-70, from September to when I went to Princeton in late August.

HB: It seems like you had a very wide range of educational experiences.

TR: Yes. I had wonderful experiences as a cab driver, most of them very positive ones. Then I went to Princeton and did my degree very quickly. I wanted to be a French historian, because of my French, and because Strayer was also a French medievalist. But when the time came to do my research, I had a wife and two kids and not enough money to live in Paris. So I went to Spain, which was cheaper.

I began my historical career as an institutional historian. I was trained by Joseph Strayer, and we wanted to know about the administration of France under Phillip IV at the end of the 13th and beginning of the 14th centuries. That's what we focused on. My first work, about Burgos and so on (*The City and the Realm: Burgos and Castile, 1080–1492*), was essentially in that vein.

But I have three great, later influences in my life, three "intellectual fathers", if you will.

Of course, none of them erase what I learned from Joseph Strayer, who was an extremely nurturing adviser. I am here because he allowed me all kinds of mistakes and supported me. He was extraordinarily kind to me and to some of the other graduate students.

At Princeton at that time—we're talking about the early 1970s—there was also a fabled English historian, Lawrence Stone, who was one of the most eclectic historians you can possibly think of. He had the ability to immediately graft himself onto any new movement that developed.

These are the years when social history was waxing very, very strongly; and at Princeton there was a seminar—which still runs—called the Davis Center seminar, which Lawrence Stone ran for twenty years.

These were hotbeds of extreme intellectual struggle, because he did not take fools very kindly. Everything was contested there, and I learned a lot about a very different kind of history. Lawrence Stone was a member of the editorial board of *Past and Present*, which represented a kind of Neo-Marxist, social history best exemplified not only by the work of Lawrence but the work of people like Rodney Hilton, Eric Hobsbawm and so forth. It was a very exciting time for me and I began to move in that direction.

Another great influence on me was Carl Schorske, for whom I served as a teaching assistant. Carl Schorske was, and is–he's still alive, although now very, very old—the best teacher I have ever seen in my life.

When people ask me, "*What do you do?*" I never tell them that I write books. I tell them that I'm a teacher—that is what I love to do. I'm coming to the end of it now, but I still love it. And Carl Schorske was the best teacher I have ever seen.

HB: What made him so fantastic?

TR: I don't teach like him, but he was incredibly keen on teaching undergraduates. It was a performance: he had music behind him and images. It was so elegant and beautiful that you were utterly seduced by it.

Lastly, there was Jacques Le Goff, to whom I became very close at the end of the 1970s. Sadly, he passed away very recently.

I was invited to France three times to run a seminar there in January, and I also sat in his seminar. He was the proponent of a kind of anthropological, social and cultural history; and somehow my work shifted in that direction as well, without ever ceasing to be a social historian.

HB: Among contemporary historians, who are the ones you find most impressive? Whom do you hold in the highest regard?

TR: Well, I should first emphasize the fact that I will naturally be mostly talking about medievalists, although I can mention some of my other colleagues as well.

Of the medievalists, I would think of someone like David Nirenberg at the University of Chicago, whose work, *Communities of Violence*, completely transformed the landscape of Iberian history.

There is Daniel Lord Smail at Harvard, whose first book, *Imaginary Cartographies* about Marseille, was absolutely amazing. He has also worked on deep history, history over a very long period of time.

Then there is Bill Jordan at Princeton, who is extremely prolific, and Paul Freedman at Yale, who is very eclectic. Paul wrote a book on the origins of peasant servitude in Catalonia and recently wrote another on spices from the East. He's a very wonderful and affable friend. And there are other people in that generation who are also remarkable.

I'm really thinking of people in the United States, but I can mention other people abroad; Peter Linehan or R.J. Moore, or Angus Mackay. At UCLA there is also Lynn Hunt or Margaret Jacob or Carlo Ginzburg, who is a historian beyond belief.

HB: What makes someone a historian beyond belief?

TR: Well, his originality. He is such an original thinker. Many years ago, from a group of documents in the Vatican Archives, he wrote a book called *I Benandanti*, in Italian—*The Night Battles* in English—which is really a remarkable anthropological study of a sect that would be declared witches by the Inquisition but who were essentially practicing some form of pre-Christian, agricultural cults. He also wrote *The Cheese and the Worms* and many, many other books that are really quite remarkable. Peter Brown at Princeton is certainly another person who should be mentioned. He's retired now, but his entire career is really, very remarkable.

HB: So, originality, creativity, insight...

TR: Yes: a volume of good things, one after another.

Questions for Discussion:

1. Do you think Teo's wide range of experiences outside of the academic world made him a better historian somehow?

2. Have you heard of, or read, any of the works Teo mentions at the end of this chapter? To what extent do you think that professional historians are sufficiently well respected by those outside of academe?

III. Historical Ruminations

Meditations on the bigger picture

HB: Let's move to some of your work in medieval history. One of the things that you explicitly mention when you discuss witchcraft and other superstitious thinking, is the curious juxtaposition of how some of the most barbaric, closed-minded movements can arise in tandem with what we now consider to be foundational movements in higher thought, such as the Enlightenment and Renaissance. How is that possible? How is it possible that these things can occur simultaneously?

TR: I think that there is definitely something to Walter Benjamin's statement that there is no monument of civilization that isn't also a monument of barbarity. It speaks to the fact that high culture—the Renaissance, the Scientific Revolution—is built upon the shoulders of the many who toil in ignorance. People like Jean Delumeau have insightfully highlighted the ways that you can channel a great deal of the anxieties of a society into these persecutory stages.

But to answer your specific question, "*How do you have periods in which you have all this incredible, cultural production accompanied by extreme persecutions of people?*"

I find that very much the pattern of historical development. We always look to the example of the Ancient Greeks as creating this world of measures and "nothing in excess" and "know thyself", but these are the same Greeks who practiced forms of misogyny which were extreme, who were a slave-holding society, who engaged in brutal kinds of imperial, colonial practices.

These are the same Athenians who exterminate people who resist them. Look at the Mytilenean Debate found in Thucydides, which is such a crude demonstration of this exercise of power.

HB: It's quite a ringing indictment of democracy as well.

TR: Yes, indeed. Then we have slaves living in absolutely abysmal conditions, working in the silver mines...

HB: Historically speaking, then, there seems to be a great distortion as we pick out the best, the most elevated, the most cultured offerings that a society has to offer: Plato stands out, Aristotle stands out, Aristophanes stands out, and so forth. But that's hardly indicative of the great masses of people who lived at the time and place, or their policies.

TR: Yes. Associated with this is a very complicated, historical question: *Are great cultural achievements built upon the toil, sacrifices and anguish of the many?*

Think about today's society and the growing level of inequality in the world. There are a few societies that have a fairly good amount of equality, good education and health systems: the Scandinavian societies, say. But, of course, they are also not welcoming to outsiders, and they are very homogeneous. They have a level of prosperity and well-being which is certainly not matched by the rest of the world.

I was lecturing in Spain not too long ago. And while I was there, we watched a scene on television where thousands of sub-Saharan Africans came across the Sahara and then amassed in woods outside the fences of Melilla, a Spanish enclave in Africa. Then, when the moment was ripe, thousands of them tried to scale the fence. Only 500 made it, and they kissed the ground and cheered, even though they had simply reached a place where they were being detained.

That's also happening in Lampedusa, the island off Sicily, as well as other places. And the discourse that I hear among my friends, people whom I think very highly of, is highly anti-immigrant: *"These people are destroying the world."*

Well, this is the point, isn't it? Why does one migrate? One migrates because one's life is almost unbearable. And until we, sort of, equal or level the playing field, people will continue to migrate.

HB: Is there any sense, in your experience, of people learning from history? Of course there's the famous quote by Santayana, about the need to learn from history in order to avoid being condemned to repeat it, but there have been many people, from Thucydides on down, who talked about why it's very important to document things.

Thucydides himself, of course, made a point of specifically highlighting things like the symptoms of diseases so that future generations might be able to specifically identify them and deal with them. But what do you think? Is it folly to even imagine learning from history?

TR: I think we do learn from history, otherwise what am I doing here? I should be teaching science-fiction or something like that. I think we do learn from history. I don't think, however, that if we don't learn from history we're going to repeat the same mistakes. History never repeats itself, although there are patterns. It's always very different. The context is always changing.

HB: But isn't that what he really meant? Isn't he saying something more metaphorical? He probably didn't mean, "repeat" literally.

TR: Yes, but essentially we don't always learn enough to avoid the mistakes. Last summer I was teaching in Paris, and, as always, I went to visit Jacques Le Goff for lunch. I was teaching a class online, and my students were reading an article by Jacques: a very famous piece on church time and merchant time, where he talks about the time when the clock was invented, when people begin to think of time as no longer belonging to God, but as something that you could make money out of ("Church time and merchant time in the Middle Ages").

I asked him if he would say something to my class, and he told me, very eloquently, that he would begin with a painting by Paul Gaugin that's in the Museum of Fine Arts in Boston, *Where Do We*

Come From? What Are We? Where Are We Going? He said, *"These are the questions that history can answer."*

I think it is important to think historically, not only because we may "avoid" some mistakes if we know the history—not that we are going to repeat the mistakes, but that we might avoid some mistakes—but it's also because we, as human beings are deeply bound by historical processes.

Even if we never understand them as such, or even care about history—perhaps because as high-school students we are convinced that history amounts to a mere memorization of dates—there are historical processes at work that led to a witch-craze in the midst of the Renaissance, or to Bacchanalia in classical Athens in the midst of the most amazing philosophical outpouring.

If we want to know who we are, where we are going and where we come from, we have to know history not as a science, but as a humanistic discipline.

I think that there is something beyond that, too. And that is that without humanities, without history and literature and so on, we cannot be, in a sense, full citizens.

Citizenship requires a kind of understanding of issues. You see how, in the political processes in this country, or in other countries, the truth is continuously distorted and the past is continuously reinvented. It's remade.

I have always been so moved by George Orwell's *1984*, because it is absolutely true: the past is always malleable. I emphasize that whenever possible to my students, that the past that they're learning in my class is one perspective, but we must learn about different interpretations of the past if we want to sort out how we are going to be full members of a democratic community, whatever that is.

HB: You said something just now that I find intriguing. You said, *"It's just one perspective."* Of course it's your perspective, but I'm also guessing that you believe, as a historian, if not in some objective Truth with a capital T, at the very least that there are things that happened and others didn't. Events may be interpreted differently, but presumably we're not talking about unbridled relativism here...

TR: Well, I had this discussion with my students on Tuesday, as it happens. When I first began doing scholarly research, I'd look at a document in the municipal archive of Burgos. I spent many months there looking at documents.

But now let's dig deeper into that: *Who wrote those documents? For what purpose are these documents written?* These documents that allow us to see that the past is also mediated by such things as basic literary skills, for example, in a society where the majority of people are illiterate.

Most of these documents are either administrative documents or having to do with transfers of property. They provide, shall we say, a written garment to something very specific, which is the nature of owning things, of relationships of power, of social distinctions and so on. How are we to see the past objectively, when the material that allows us to see the past is necessarily clouded by these structures?

On the other hand, I am a historian. I mean, this is the great challenge that postmodern theory posed for historians: *If language is unstable, how could you know anything that happened?*

As a historian, I say, *"No, no. There **is** something you can know."* But no well-trained historian today will look at the past in the same fashion that we did 30 years ago. We will be more critical of our sources, we will try to find alternate points of views, and so forth.

HB: That strikes me as almost an argument for why we have to keep training historians, because 30 years hence, there will be historians who naturally look at the world differently from the way we look at the world today.

TR: Absolutely. Every ten years we rewrite the past. Unfortunately, the number of historians will be less. Not only here, but in France and Spain and so on, because all the departments of history are contracting in these countries, with the exception of some extremely wealthy places that can afford to have them.

Less graduate students have been admitted to history programs, there is a defunding of the humanities and the social sciences that is going on here and elsewhere in the Western world. Languages are being eliminated from the curriculum, except for a few languages such as Spanish and Chinese and Arabic for a combination of practical reasons: the realities of living in the United States, the economic power of China, and for strategic, geopolitical reasons.

I'll give you an example: not too long ago, an "intellectual massacre" took place at SUNY Albany that has become paradigmatic. It's not exceptional. It has been happening, to a lesser degree, elsewhere. They decided that, for the sake of economy, they would close down the departments of German, French, Italian and Classics. And they let all the faculty go.

So let's say you are a parent and you send your child to study at SUNY Albany and she wants to be a historian of France or Germany. There is no way she can learn the language. The languages might be taught in a service capacity here and there, but she cannot learn the literature. So then she will naturally choose to do US history or Spanish history or Chinese history.

This is a common trend. There's a kind of attack on the humanities and the social sciences, which is widespread throughout the Western world, in which the opportunities to enter the profession are far less than they were when I was young.

HB: I'm still thinking about how, concretely, we can best harness historical understanding. I'm wondering if it's possible to point concretely to any instances where we can say, "*Oh yes, we as a society appreciated this historical event. We didn't go here. We went there instead, because we realized, 'Uh-oh, that way lies madness; we've done that before'.*" Can we point to any concrete examples of that, you think?

TR: Well, I don't know that we can actually point out one event where a society said, "*We didn't do this because we suffered in the past.*" But I could give you one example that roughly reflects this: the great crash of 1929. This disaster clearly caught everybody by surprise, but we came very close in 2008 to something like that—a crash that was inspired by a few people at the top who make huge amounts of money out of the miseries of the world. It's very clear that governments immediately reacted to the crisis.

HB: Ben Bernanke was actually a student of the 1929 crash, as I understand it.

TR: Yes. They didn't react perhaps in the ways in which we think they should have reacted, but nonetheless there was a sense that there are certain things you cannot allow. You cannot allow the financial sector to collapse. The Chinese invested trillions of dollars in infrastructure as a way to combat the declining business. So there is an example where people's knowledge of the past and knowledge of the mechanics of economic change had an impact.

We can enter into a debate about whether or not it was all that could have been done. Personally, I think it was not enough and it was channelled into some very specific sectors rather than other sectors, but that's another discussion.

Let me give you another example. There was 9/11, with two wars resulting from that. Any historian would have told you that Iraq is a deeply divided sectarian society that was only held together by a savage dictator.

George H.W. Bush understood this in ways his son did not. Bush's father did not go in, recognizing that there was not going to be a reception committee with flowers waiting for you.

In the same fashion, history could tell us that Afghanistan is a really difficult place to ever control: Alexander failed, the British failed, the Russians failed and the Americans failed too, because if there are gains there, they are very limited ones. It is a tribal society. There is no civil society at all. It's a deeply religious society. How do you control this? *"We are going to bomb you to the Stone Age?"* They're already in the Stone Age. What are you going to do? There are no targets there.

And yet, after ten years of it, which have cost—what? a billion dollars every month?—what have we actually accomplished?

HB: Does history give us any more concrete guide in terms of what we might do other than, *"There are some real difficulties here: Alexander tried, the Russians tried, and so forth."*

Let me be more specific, let's talk a little bit about Afghanistan. From the position of an American, there seemed to be a clear reason to act back in 2001. There was a country filled with areas to train people to launch terrorist attacks against America.

It seems to me that if I'm in charge of US defense policy, I don't have many deliberations to make. I say, *"We have to make sure that doesn't happen again; we have to take preventative measures."*

It's true, of course, that this is a fragmented society which is suppressed by extremely retrograde, fundamentalist, misogynistic people; and, as we go in to destroy a terrorist infrastructure to do our best to ensure our own safety against future attacks, we should somehow consider how best to do our part to contribute towards the evolution of this country in a more progressive way.

Notwithstanding all these difficulties that you mentioned, does history give us any clear guide as to what we should do other than, *"Beware. Many have tried to invade this place and it didn't work"*?

TR: It's the geopolitics of the whole thing. The Russians have yearned for Afghanistan for centuries: it's their access to India and the Indian Ocean. The ten-years invasion of Afghanistan by the Russians was not something that came out of nowhere.

There are no easy answers, ever. As you say, this is the place where the attacks came from. Al Qaeda had deeply rooted itself into the area. I don't have answers to this. It's clear that there has been some progress in the quest to develop a civil society—I was reading today about the number of women who were involved in meetings, and there were some women running for office as well—but how deep is our involvement there? After all, the Americans had long been involved in Afghanistan: they supported the Taliban against the Russians because, *"the enemies of my enemies are my friends."*

HB: I'm not holding a brief for American foreign policy. I'm just looking for a specific situation where a historian can provide valuable advice. And it seems to me the advice of, "*Well, this is a potentially unconquerable country because other regimes have tried to conquer it*," only goes so far.

TR: It is a potentially unconquerable country because of the fragmented nature of the society, not because other countries have failed, but because there is no hold. You know, the European tradition in which you can defeat an army and then the capital surrenders and you're given the keys to the city—*The Surrender of Breda*, say, as painted by Velasquez, with all of its pomp and courtesy—doesn't actually work in history.

The Russians proved that, twice. They will not surrender. They will suck you in, and eventually they will kill you. They did it to Napoleon, they did it to the Nazis. So, there are societies in which there is no centre. Capturing Kabul and putting in a figurehead who is corrupt and has all these tribal affiliations, in a country that is deeply fractured with different tribal societies, simply will not work.

There is a very interesting film, a surprising film, called *The Beast of War*. It's an American movie about a valley in Afghanistan where a Russian tank that has just destroyed a Pashtun village gets separated from its main group. This valley has only one exit, and the tank becomes lost in this valley and has nowhere to go. Then the Pashtuns come out to hunt the tank.

It is a surprising film, because it is also a film that gives you a lens through which you can look at historical processes that are not necessarily in books but are about the passions that agitate humans. At the end, it is almost a kind of glorification of this drive of these tribal people towards revenge. They didn't care that these Russians were communists any more than they care that Americans are democrats. It was simply, "*You destroyed my village. You killed my relatives. I'm going to come after you.*"

It's really a remarkable film because the Russians themselves are ambivalent. Some are gung-ho, while others are saying, "*What are we doing here? This is total insanity.*" Some are friendly to the Afghans or the Pashtuns, and some are not. In the very traditional fashion, they even had a member of the Afghan army with them, serving as a kind of go-between and interlocutor.

So, I do not know what a historian can tell a politician with regards to the best way to approach dealing with Afghanistan or Iraq or Crimea or Ukraine or anything like that. But historians can point out that it's not so simple. It's never simple, because if you understand the history, and you understand those webs of significance that exist there—to use Clifford Geertz, again—then you will see another world.

We are all in our little caves and we are very different from each other. Sometimes we can go into other caves and see the other people, but we don't fully understand them ever; and therefore we have to be aware of this.

And that's what history, in a sense, can teach us.

Questions for Discussion:

1. Teo says that, *"if we want to know who we are, where we are going and where we come from, we have to know history not as a science, but as a humanistic discipline."* To what extent can history be viewed as *"a science"* at all?

2. How does Teo's invocation of the painting *The Surrender of Breda* illustrate how the astute historian can help minimize the damaging effect of political propaganda?

3. Do we have, on the whole, sufficient knowledge of history in order for our contemporary society to successfully learn from it?

IV. Progress?

Weighed down by "the human condition"?

HB: Listening to you, there seems to be a sense of tension between the constancy of human nature and a sense of progress. Let me try to be a little bit more specific, taking your recent example, *"You're in my village, you've hurt my people, I'm going to get you."*

This is a very tribal, basic response that one can imagine has played out for thousands of years ever since there have been human tribes: protecting one's own, an eye for an eye, and so forth.

On the other hand, if one looks at human civilization and takes the long view, clearly the society in which we currently find ourselves is very different than societies of a thousand years ago or even five hundred years ago.

As a professional historian, do you find that there is a constant give and take in evaluating societies between saying, *"This is very different than another time and place,"* or *"This is merely the present version, the most recent instantiation of these standard human characteristics"*? Do you go back and forth? How do you look at that?

TR: You know, I think that each moment, each context, yields or produces a very different outcome that is essentially bound and tied to all kinds of things, which are not always easy to determine. Are we the same as early hominids fighting in tribes?

I teach a class on world history from the beginning to 500. And in my last class, last fall, a student built a computer model in which you could see whether you would survive or become extinct.

You find somebody who is suffering from smallpox, do you try to cure her? Do you isolate her? Or do you kill her? And, depending on the variables, you end up reproducing or dying.

It's not always easy because each condition varies. I have my very serious doubts about the idea of progress. Are we more civilized today than we were a thousand years ago? Probably. Do we have more technology at our hands? Probably. As a group, not as individuals who vary immensely, are we more tolerant? Probably.

But, that does not mean that the human reaction to, *You have killed somebody in my village and I have to get you,* has changed all that much.

That is precisely what happened after 9/11. I traveled to New York from Los Angeles in one of the first flights going back. I walked to the site. I walked back to Union Square, which was filled with signs saying, *Time for Peace, We Must Forgive.*

There was a sense that we must understand the elements that prompted this kind of behaviour and action, but that did not last because it is so easy to manipulate this justified anger. It is so easy to forget.

We lost more than 3,400 people in the World Trade Center and other terrorist attacks—which is, of course, 3,400 too many—but then, how many have died in an attempt to get payback for this? How many? Over 100,000 people in Iraq, with close to 5,000 American soldiers.

We do this all the time. In the 21st century, sophisticated people that we are, enlightened people with access to all kinds of technologies, killing has become much easier. It's so easy to kill someone with a drone, you don't see the people who die. Technological progress has also made possible carnage in ways that were unthinkable.

The 20th century was one of the most brutal centuries in all of mankind. I cannot even think of anything that comes close to this, beginning with the Armenian genocide, the First World War, the gulags of Stalin, the destruction of Guernica during the Spanish Civil War as a way of testing the possibility of terror bombing, the Second World War and the Holocaust—which is a chapter in itself—the atomic bombing of Hiroshima and Nagasaki, the Cambodian massacres, the genocide in Rwanda...

All of this happened in the 20th century, the century that also gave us television, computers and cellphones.

HB: In terms of progress, then, it's an open question, to put it mildly.

TR: Yes. In terms of progress, Nietzsche traced this first. Have we progressed as humans? Are we kinder, nicer? Probably we are kinder and nicer, certainly to those around us. But the same person who is very kind and nice will spend millions of dollars campaigning to block immigrants from entering this country or Europe, or to make sure that people cannot marry if they have the same gender, or that women do not have abortions.

HB: In *The Terror of History*, but also in other books, you talk about the relationship between religion and power. Has that changed substantially, you think? Is it evolving?

Taking the long view, are we now at a stage where we can say, "*Yes, it's true that religion and power have long been deeply intertwined, but now we have the formal separation of church and state, at least in some parts of the world; we have an understanding of the dangers there and we've made some kind of objective progress in terms of a separation of these two things.*"

Do you agree with that perspective?

TR: It is true that in some advanced societies, the link between religion and politics has been severed. Again, I'm referring here to Scandinavian societies. It is true that there are also countries, such as France, which are exceedingly secular, despite the fact that 11% of the population is now Muslim and there are obvious tensions there.

HB: It's a proudly secular society. They constantly refer to the 1905 legislation that officially separated church and state.

TR: Yes. And it's clear that in places like England, the church has lost all of its relevance, even though there are fundamentalist groups among Muslim inhabitants of England. So it is evident that, in some places, the role of religion has diminished.

There are other places, however, where religion plays a significant role in terms of politics—the United States, for example—and yet there are developments that are inconceivable and impossible to have been predicted by historians.

For example, the attitude towards homosexuality in these societies has dramatically been transformed in a period of ten years. Why? How does that happen? Twelve years ago, some politicians ran on an anti-homosexual platform, and now, suddenly, nobody gives a hoot about this except for some crazies.

HB: Marijuana legalization, as well. I didn't see that one coming.

TR: Exactly. How does that happen? So, there are social issues that have moved very quickly, where others have not: immigration, religion, and so forth. The United States is a deeply religious country—at least half of it is deeply religious.

I actually truly believe that the great enemies of mankind are nationalism and religion, and that most wars have been fought either by people who argue that, "*My country needs to expand,*" or "*It's better than yours,*" or by people who said, "*You are not of my own religion, therefore I have the right to kill you.*"

HB: Or both.

TR: Or both. Often both. In World War One, the German bishops prayed to God for a German victory and the French bishops prayed to God for a French victory.

HB: So, the way I look at it—let me just posit my view and you can react. I certainly see that humans are these very selfish, retributive, horrible beings that act in very horrific ways towards one another, but there are some things that do seem to have changed for the better on a sociological level.

Many countries around the world are democracies, more or less.

There is an opportunity for most people to at least express themselves. There is, perhaps more significantly, an opportunity for power to change, so you don't get this entrenched sense of power and accompanying oligarchies.

You don't have these unelected, religious bodies playing the formative role that they used to play in terms of guiding societies and guiding policies. I don't look at myself as a wide-eyed optimist, by and large, but you're a medieval historian: if I ask myself if I'd rather live in medieval times or now, I don't have a hugely complicated decision to make.

TR: No, no: I tell my students, *"Don't glorify the Middle Ages."* The Middle Ages was a terrible period. Most people died very early and lived very miserable lives. Only the very few at the top lived somewhat acceptable lives; and that was not very good either.

HB: So, I don't want to glorify the past, and I don't want to think that we're living in this wonderful age now, but it does seem that, objectively speaking, there has been some sense of progress.

TR: There is some sense of progress. The reality is that there are many societies around the world where the quality of life is very good. People get educated. They get health insurance in most civilized countries. They have political participation. There is redistribution of wealth in at least some countries while not much in others.

However, having said that, the developments that date to the current economic crisis—but which have been growing for quite a long time—are alarming, because one of the things that is very obvious is the growing inequality between social classes.

Recently, I read a review of a book written by a Frenchman, of all things, in which he looked at all the economic data over a hundred years. And his final conclusion was that inequality is growing, rather than decreasing.

HB: This is globally, I presume.

TR: Yes, globally. Democracy's great promise was that it was going to, in a sense, level the playing field. And that is not true. I haven't read the book yet, and I don't know the details of his argument.

But I took the review article with me when I was leaving that morning for Spain, and I later decided to cut it out and put it on my door, because it's a very alarming situation. Will the world in which I grew up exist in the next 10, 15, 20 years?

I am perhaps a bit of a pessimist in this, but I don't think it will. My granddaughter is going to do very well, I hope. I'm putting money away for her like crazy. But will she have the same opportunities that I had? I don't think so.

HB: There's the question of how best to equip ourselves with the right tools to be able to answer that question. And this, in turn, leads to your motivation, I would imagine, to not only teach, but also, within a broader context, to learn about history, to appreciate history.

I have been going on for some time probing you about the question of how we might harness our knowledge of historical progress for some direct societal benefit: *Are we learning from history? Can we actually move forwards coherently, with the full benefit imparted to us of past events and circumstances?*

There is, as we've said, the more direct, quasi-simplistic, assessment: "*I am the President of the United States and I noticed in the past that we went down this road and that didn't work out very well because I know my history, so maybe we should take this approach now instead.*"

Whether things can ever be boiled down that simply is very much a dubious question, but at least, in theory, it's possible to imagine history being able to be applied directly.

However, there are, of course, indirect ways of applying our knowledge of history, and the humanities in general. There is this notion that, by learning about past societies, by learning about what other people have written about their ambitions, their goals, their desires, their frustrations, by getting a deeper perspective of historical context—different cultures, different societies, the human condition—we elevate ourselves and equip ourselves with the tools to be able to make more sophisticated judgments, to be able to make more balanced and tolerant and insightful judgments about present-day situations that no one could have possibly prepared us for.

Is that a key aspect or a key framework that you rely upon when you want to teach history? Do you look at history that way, or do you look at it in a different context altogether?

TR: No, I think I do it like this. What I want to do when I teach, particularly undergraduates—which is a very different sort of training than for graduate students which is inevitably much more navel-gazing oriented—is to do what you have just so clearly described.

But I also want them to understand something else. These are 18 or 19-year-old kids who, for the most part, have not reflected very much on existential questions concerning the meaning of life, or anything like that.

I always say to them, *"Don't think of yourself as the final product of an evolutionary and historical process that culminates with you. These people living in the first or fifth century in India or China, or in the 12th or 16th century in France or Spain, were facing issues not so different from the ones that you may be facing. Here is how they tried to get through their lives and their difficult periods. Their answers are not always right. They may have consequences that lead to awful things. But these are people who are alive."*

This is something that I said too in *The Terror of History*. I want to convey to my students the fact that many of these people who wrote, or who lived, or who were peasants in a village—which I had tried to at least name, to bring them back to life—are as alive as many of us, because they live on in our memory and our consciousness, because we read them, because we are moved by the way they wrote, because we adore the music they wrote or the paintings they made.

These are not cultural products that you somehow own, these are cultural products that serve as a link to all humans who lived before you. You must understand that these wonderful, cultural trophies, as Walter Benjamin once said, are always paid with a terrible, terrible price.

The Industrial Revolution—which I used to teach, but have not taught for many years—this unique moment in which places, like England and the Netherlands, then Germany and France, catapult into great, global dominance, a dominance that is paid for by their workers in those satanic mills that Blake described so vividly—

HB: But who are otherwise, at least individually, largely forgotten.

TR: Yes. And, of course, there is an end to this. There is a way in which societies kind of settle, and then workers begin to struggle for their rights and gain a series of benefits through unions and so on. But all that is gone. It's now been rolled back. 150-200 years of struggle of the working class to gain a foothold and a share of the pie have now been rolled back.

HB: As you say, the global increase in inequality seems to indicate that the values that people used to subscribe to are, at best, being held somewhat indifferently, in terms of where we are going as a society.

Questions for Discussion:

1. If you could choose to live in any historical period, which one would it be and why?

2. Do you agree with Walter Benjamin's sentiment cited by Teo that "these wonderful cultural trophies are always paid with a terrible, terrible price"? Does it follow that if we're not, generally speaking, "paying a terrible price", we are not likely to produce "wonderful cultural trophies"?

V. Connecting

Technology and personal factors

HB: I'd like to ask you about technology, and how it relates to the way people look at the past.

Obviously I'm not a historian, and I don't teach people history, but I could imagine that undergraduates today, as technology improves, have an increasingly patronizing view of the past, related to what you were saying a moment ago about looking at themselves as the endpoint of some evolutionary and historical process: "*Oh, those poor people, they didn't have cellphones, they couldn't take pictures, they were so backwards.*"

In other words, I can imagine that technology itself plays a significant role in intuitively distancing today's students from those who lived in another time, making it harder to regard them as being fully flesh-and-blood people with desires and dreams and wishes and hopes just like us. Is that a fair statement?

TR: I think so. I am actually not unhappy to be the age that I am. I love my undergraduates. I teach because I also love the students: there is something that happens in the classroom—not always, but sometimes—there is a moment of recognition, the moment when a life is transformed.

But I am glad that I am the age that I am, when the end is near, both of my teaching and of my life, because I think that for the first time we are teaching a generation that has completely grown up in a technologically-shaped world.

It's not that they don't know anything or that they are stupid. But they don't know the things I know, they don't have the same frames of reference that I have, they don't really share a common culture with me.

They know other things that I do not know. Am I being antiquarian? Am I being an ultra-reactionary who still thinks that there is value to knowing poetry or knowing history?

Because, after all, you don't need my class. You can just Google anything, and it comes up, right there, right away. You get to a Wikipedia page, which may be true or not.

HB: Is it possible to connect with them? Can you get beyond that?

My guess is, from the passion and the love that you've clearly demonstrated both for your students and for the art of teaching in general, that notwithstanding their background, notwithstanding all the technology that they have grown up with which separates them from you culturally, that when you encounter them, you are able to inspire them, you are able to tell them stories of human drama and the human condition, you are able to make people from medieval times seem real and relevant to them.

TR: Perhaps to some. But in general, I think this relates back to the kinds of things that we were talking about earlier, the nature of language and things like that. I think that there has been a tremendous shift in the manner in which people learn, both how they learn and what they learn.

So, yes, I might inspire them. Generally speaking, they love my classes and give me wonderful evaluations, because they know that I care for them. I bring passion and get rhetorically inspired in the classroom. But I also know that they might just like the messenger, but not necessarily the message.

HB: So, you don't get the sense that when they're out of the classroom and there's no longer Professor Ruiz to inspire them or stimulate them that they're going to pick up a copy of, say, Montaigne's essays?

TR: You hope that in the future they will. Not now, perhaps: they are only 18 and 19 and there is such pressure to succeed, such pressure to get good grades so they can go to law school or medical school or whatever, such pressure for job acquisition that learning for the extraordinary pleasure of learning is not even considered.

I mean, why do I do this? I do this because sometime in my life I got caught up with certain things: with reading, with appreciating certain things.

Such an attitude still occurs these days, but it's not common.

I also think this has to do with these new ways of learning. Something may have happened to the neural connections, the synapses in the brain. My granddaughter is only eight years old and she has had an iPad already for two years.

HB: *You* didn't give it to her, did you?

TR: Yes, I gave it to her. I'm a grandfather.

HB: *You* gave it to her? Oh, my goodness. You're part of the problem, man.

TR: I know, I know. I'm complicit. I'm totally complicit.

But she designs things with it and sends them to me—it's all very lovely. She's had *Harry Potter* read to her. But that seems increasingly rare to me. When I have a small class, I give all my students a little index card and I say to them, "*Give me your name, email, major, the last book you read for fun and the last movie you saw for fun.*"

I sometimes get surprising things, like, "*I read this play by Camus.*" But the truth of the matter is that I bet 99% of the books that were "read for fun" were books that were actually assigned for some class.

Yet, on the other hand, I also teach a one-credit Fiat Lux course at UCLA, on *Pride and Prejudice* and the social world of Jane Austen. I get twenty students, mostly women, who are all absolutely ferocious readers of Jane Austen. They know the book backwards and forwards, they challenge me on the things that I don't remember about the book. There is a kind of relationship to reading that clearly exists there.

The question is, how do we make this part and parcel of the world in which we live? How do we inspire people?

The Terror of History has a very pessimistic ending, but there's also an avowal that this is what we do with our lives: we embrace certain things that give us extraordinary rewards, and most of them are through art and through learning and through literature.

There is a book that I mentioned in *The Terror of History*, a book that impressed me to no end: Bruce Duffy's *The World As I Found It*.

It's a fictionalized description of the relationship between Bertrand Russell, G.E. Moore and Ludwig Wittgenstein. It's a powerful, heartfelt book about these three people grasping to make sense of the world.

And, at the end, we are trying to do the same thing: to make sense of the world. And that's what I want to tell the students.

OK, don't necessarily do it at 18. Go and have a ball now. But sometime or another, you have to really take stock of yourself and try to see how you make sense of the world, and of yourself in that world.

HB: Another interesting aspect of history, and the humanities in general, is that one has a sense that it's tied much more directly to one's personal development.

It's certainly possible to pick up a book on, say, quantum field theory, in your forties after not having had a rigorous education in physics—the information is certainly out there. However, it's highly unlikely that many people will do that. There's an understanding that when you're 18 or 19, when you're in your formative years, you get a certain training and then go off in a certain direction, which is either scientific or it's not.

History seems different to me in this respect. There is a certain hope, if not actual expectation, that those who were exposed to it at university will be sufficiently stimulated, as you say, to continue to read history throughout their lives. And there's also a hope that people who may not have been history majors at university will also begin to engage in the historical process and be stimulated by the subject when they get older.

You spoke just now of encouraging 18 and 19 year olds to "go out and have a ball", which seems reasonable—after all, when you're 18, you've got rather different priorities in life. But do you nonetheless teach explicitly with the idea that this is a lifelong pursuit, a lifelong intellectual development?

TR: Yes; and it is very rewarding when they write to you, 20–30 years afterwards, and say, *"I'll always remember this."* Many become lawyers, say, but have this passion for history and really wish they could have been historians except that they couldn't bear the thought of making such low salaries. So, there is an impact, there is a kind of gain there.

I don't think I teach at the same level in all classes, however: the topic determines how I teach. For example, in the class on world history, which is an entering class for freshmen, my only purpose is to offer a position of dissent to the unreflective Western bias, to point out that some of these ideas that they so cherish, that they think are original, really originated elsewhere, in Asia, in India, in China. Five hundred years before Jesus, somebody was saying exactly the same thing, except that he is saying it from a secular point of view: no God involved.

I always ask the students the very simple question, *"What year is it?"* And when they tell me, I ask them, *"Why?"*

They never understand that chronology is an articulation of power, that we talk about being in the year "2014" because the West won. If China had won in the 19th century, say, if we would find ourselves in a world that was not Eurocentric or Western-centric, then we would have a very different calendar: these things are arbitrary impositions of power.

This is something that I always insist upon in the class: there are no universal values. *"Oh yes, yes, there is God,"* they will tell me. Well, not really. A billion and a half Chinese are animistic, they believe in ancestor worship. Sometimes there is nothing at all: there are entire civilizations that have no god.

HB: So, let me interject for a moment—not so much on religious grounds, but on this question of whether or not it makes sense to talk about universal human values as we now understand them.

Whether or not these are truly universal is a question I'm not even going to attempt to address, but de facto, the Universal Declaration of Human Rights, say, is precisely that—universal—because virtually all countries have signed on to it.

So we can now say that there are some things that we, at least on a near-universal level throughout present-day humanity, acknowledge should be done, even if we don't actually do them.

TR: But the truth of the matter, of course, is that that is also something that can be questioned. Let's imagine that the Aztecs would have conquered the world. They engaged in human sacrifices and symbolic wars where they capture people and execute them. Is that system unethical for the Aztecs, or does it make perfect sense?

So, the West won. We have a philosophical tradition that was born in the 18th century, which is part of the Judeo-Christian, Arabic tradition. We passed The Declaration of the Rights of Man and the Citizen in France in 1789.

So, I am not saying that sacrificing people is good...

HB: No, I understand. You're simply looking at different human societies and different times.

TR: Yes. And each of these cultures or societies has a system that essentially organizes their lives, and it's perfectly rational. It's only when in contact with other systems and contestations of power that one system essentially overwhelms the other and imposes its values.

Do we think that murdering ten million people is good? Of course not, it's awful. This is the ultimate horror.

But it is true that the West established a system of values that is then imposed upon the rest of the world in order to give itself ethical supremacy over others: "*I am better than you because I am a Christian and you are a Polytheist, and therefore I have the right to conquer you.*"

Questions for Discussion:

1. Does modern technology increase, decrease, or have no effect on our ability to culturally flourish?

2. Would you describe Teo as a "cultural relativist"?

VI. Looking Ahead
Pondering history's future

HB: Let's talk for a moment about the evolution of historical research too. As you know, I had a conversation with John Elliott a little while ago, and he was telling me how the world of research has changed as a result of technology: that going into the archives and having physical contact with original documents, being able to smell and touch that world and interact in a personal way with the primary source material, that way of life as a researcher seems to be disappearing. He pointed out that there are some advantages to technology, in particular technology now exists where ink stains can be removed, say—

TR: Or you can see right through a palimpsest: using NASA technology, you can actually read the document underneath.

HB: Right. So, these are obvious advantages from a historian's point of view. But in the meantime, he expressed regret that the old days of being forced to immerse yourself in that environment, to be somehow inhaling the air associated with a certain place and time is no longer. Do you concur with that?

TR: Absolutely, completely. I should add that John Elliott, whom I met in 1975, had a tremendous influence on me. He is a man of extreme generosity. I am a great admirer of John's.

In this case, as in others, he is absolutely right. As I told you earlier, I was not always planning to be a researcher or a writer of books and articles. I became so at Princeton, when Joseph Strayer took me to the special collection and gave me a Norman charter.

Suddenly, I could touch it, I could feel the past. I could barely read it, but it was like touching something that was alive through time.

These days, my entire doctoral dissertation could have been written without leaving the apartment. Everything that I looked at or read for my dissertation is now either published or digitalized. If you now go to the General Archive of the Crown of Aragon, which is the biggest medieval archive in Europe, most of the documents would not be given to you—you would only be given access to a digital copy.

You could actually see it better in a digital form: you can make it bigger, you could read it more easily. But something is lost in translation here, because we no longer have that kind of feel of the past that is so significant and important for medievalists.

HB: With respect to your research, were there things that surprised you when you began?

TR: Medievalists especially, but some other historians as well, always go through the same shock. It happens in two ways.

The first shock is that you find a book that seems to have done what you are going to do. In the end, you adjust. I did a very different kind of dissertation from that book, but it was there, and it was very scary.

The second shock happens when you first enter the archives. You have read manuscripts back in Princeton, you have gone through paleography, and when you first arrive in the archives, you see the manuscript and you cannot read anything.

With the exception of some people who are very gifted, it's always the same story: you arrive there and you cannot make head or tail of anything. I was there for two weeks and not getting through anything. So I went to Madrid and met some friends and had a great time. And then I went back and I could read it.

It takes time for you to begin to understand the hand—these documents are done by professional scribes, who are often writing quickly. It takes time to reconstruct what is being said, word by word. But finally you can read it without any difficulties.

Most medievalists, I would say 95% of us, have this experience the first time we go to the archives.

HB: It must have been terribly deflating. You finally get to this big point in your life, you fly all the way over there...

TR: I said to myself, "*OK, you can always go back to driving a cab in New York.*" It was terrifying. Finally, I went back to the archives, and it became something that I could do.

HB: But nobody told you that this might happen.

TR: *Nobody* told me. But I tell it to all my students: it's normal not to be able to make sense of it. Mostly because there's a lot of abbreviations, and until you begin to grasp the abbreviations, you're lost.

So, what I do now to the students is I give them a document, and then I give them a printed version of the document, and the translation of the printed version so that they can see it all and compare for themselves. If I didn't do that they would come back and say, "*I cannot do this.*"

HB: The experience of supervising other people to do their research, is that something that you enjoy as much as undergraduate teaching? I get the sense that your real passion lies with teaching the undergraduates and stimulating them.

TR: Absolutely. I hate to say this in case some graduate students read this. I should say that I have been very fortunate with my choice of graduate students. I have not trained a lot of people—Strayer trained one person a year, and I have been, more or less, pretty close to that myself—so I have not trained an immense number of students.

Almost all of them have been wonderful people to work with, people I really like. Some of them are utterly brilliant, and more professional than I was myself at that level. There is a professionalization of the discipline that is very different from the way it was.

HB: How so? In terms of specialization?

TR: Specialization, certainly, but also the tools that they have, the training and expectations. Since the market is so competitive, getting into graduate school is so competitive, getting into the job market is so competitive, there's a kind of Darwinian world out there.

I see it when I read applications for fellowships. There are 33 candidates for the same fellowship that I got in 1979. I look at these applications and think to myself, *I would be number 34 here*. I'm not being modest about this; it's absolutely true. People today are far better trained than I was.

HB: Well, that is something to put on the positive side of the ledger—we were talking before about some of the negative things.

TR: Yes. Essentially what's happened is that we have become far more professional. What is expected of you has increased dramatically from the past.

HB: Does that manifest itself sometimes by too much specialization? I could imagine that, in the past, when one didn't need quite as much specialization, one could make connections to different areas—one might have had a wider, general culture, general knowledge to draw from. You know, it's the old academic saw that as you go up the food chain, you know more and more about less and less until you know everything about nothing.

TR: While there are exceptions, there are people who are polymaths and know many different things, I think that, on the whole, this relates back to a conversation we had before—which I think was not on tape—about historians writing for each other as opposed to historians writing for a wider public.

I think that we have become so specialized that we do generally know less and less about other areas, and more and more about this narrow world in which we move. I have been doing this for 41 years, so I know a lot of stuff. But I don't know it in-depth, but superficially. I can speak about any topic, but I am not an expert in any of them.

Now, people really know one thing, and there's a clash. Most of the jobs are in small colleges, where you are going to be a generalist, you are going to do many different things.

So, there are two things happening: in the first case, our training is very narrow. But on the other hand, the demands of the market inevitably force historians to do something well outside their specialty.

For example, medievalists are expected to do world history or Western civilization in a small college because there are very few faculty and you have to cover the field.

HB: That's a big ambit, though: for a medievalist to have to cover world history.

TR: Yes. World history is the most desired second field that employers want in the job market today.

I have one student now in the job market who did all the research for a seventh-grade lesson on world history. There are new standards in California, and in the seventh grade they learn about something that we call *Sites of Encounter*: places where different civilizations come together—Sicily, for example, where Muslims, Greeks, Normans, Christians, Jews and so forth lived together.

He has done research for that, which can only be of help, because he can now go into the job market and say that he also knows all about that material. But his thesis is on language shifting in the Crown of Aragon in the 12th and 13th centuries: why some people write in Latin and why some people write in the vernacular.

HB: Interesting. But I cut you off when you were comparing your desire and passion for undergraduate teaching with that of graduate supervision and teaching.

TR: This is my problem, it has nothing really to do with undergraduates. I have a very strong memory of a graduate seminar at Princeton, which was done by a legendary figure named Felix Gilbert: a great historian and scholar, a German refugee at the Institute for Advanced Study.

That was a seminar in which he did not say anything; and yet he was able to get everybody discussing. I find myself frustrated by how much I talk in my seminars. Even though I love to talk, I don't want to talk in a graduate seminar. It's much better to get others to do the talking.

HB: Is there a certain temperament that medievalists have? Can you walk down the street and say, "*There's a medievalist*"? Are there certain characteristics that somehow can be classified with medievalists?

TR: Until recently, we would have said that it was the need for linguistic and paleographical skills that sets medievalists apart. But then, if you ask an ancient historian he would say, "*Oh no, no, no. We know more languages than you do.*" Someone like Peter Brown, who reads Syrian and Greek and—well, you name it, he reads it.

HB: In terms of disposition, though, can you make any broad characterizations within the field and say, "*This guy's got an antique mindset, this one has a medieval mindset*"?

TR: No, we come in all flavours.

HB: Were you ever tempted to move to other areas?

TR: I have. I began as a medievalist, but now I do early modern work as well. That's not much of a change, but I moved into the 16th century. I actually do not believe that the distinctions between medieval and early modern hold water, so I always do a history that crosses the 1500 barrier. Although I must confess that the only original research I have done has been on the Middle Ages.

Twice I have thought very seriously about changing my career. The first time I thought of becoming a counsellor. I wanted to go and get an MSW and do counselling, until somebody told me, "*You'll do more good as a teacher talking to them.*" That may well not be a generally true statement, but I think it probably was true for me.

The other time that I thought seriously about changing careers was when I again considered teaching in secondary or primary school. It's too late now, but I think I would have liked that.

HB: Have you done any volunteer work related to teaching in schools?

TR: There is an office here in the history department that works with public schools and I talk to teachers of primary schools and help them sometimes with training. I also sponsor historical fiction, young-adult writers, to come and talk to the kids, as well as to undergraduates and graduates who want to write historical fiction.

HB: When you talk about training teachers, what do you say to them? How does that work?

TR: Well, the teachers in primary and secondary school are pretty constrained regarding the kinds of things that they can do in the classroom—they have a lesson plan that they have to follow. So this is a kind of enrichment program for teachers. Suppose that they are going to be talking about the opening of the Atlantic. I might go and give a lecture to them about how they should be teaching this topic.

Next week, for example, the medieval academy meets here, and I am sponsoring two sessions of seventh-grade teachers who are going to come. I'm going to present a demonstration on these lesson plans I spoke about earlier, on *Sites of Encounter*.

HB: And when you talk to people who are writing historical fiction, do you talk more about the historical process per se, or is it more about specific medieval details if they're interested in setting a novel in a particular time and place?

TR: I think it's more about making sure the context is right. There is a particular case of a wonderful, young-adult fiction writer, whose name is Avi. He has written and published a great deal and is very successful.

He saw one of my recorded lectures, and got the idea of writing a novel about an English boy in 1381 during the peasant uprising. And he wrote to me and said that he was writing this young-adult fiction book and asked if I would like to take a look at the final product.

He sent it to me and it was pretty accurate. I made some tiny fixes here and there, and he ended up dedicating the book to me. It's called *Crispin: The Cross of Lead* and it won the 2003 Newbery Medal for children's literature. So that's something that I'm very proud of.

HB: So history lives and thrives, despite all sociological pressures to the contrary.

TR: I certainly hope so.

HB: Teo, it's been a great pleasure talking to you today. Thank you very much.

TR: A great pleasure, Howard. Thank you.

Questions for Discussion:

1. How can the dangers of overspecialization that Teo mentions in this chapter be overcome?

2. If you could wave a magic wand and become a professional historian, which time and place would you focus on and why?

Continuing the Conversation

Readers who enjoyed this conversation are referred to Teo's book, *The Terror of History: On the Uncertainties of Life in Western Civilization* as well as his lectures: *Terror of History: Mystics, Heretics, and Witches in the Western Tradition* offered by *The Great Courses*. Those interested in his research insights on medieval Spain are directed to, for example, *From Heaven to Earth: The Reordering of Castilian Society, 1150–1350*, *Spain's Centuries of Crisis: 1300–1474* and *Spanish Society*, 1348–1700.

Herculaneum Uncovered

A conversation with Andrew Wallace-Hadrill

Introduction
Historical Value

Looked at through the eyes of an archaeologist, human catastrophes can take on a rather different hue.

When Mount Vesuvius erupted in 79 CE, it swiftly engulfed the nearby cities of Pompeii and Herculaneum in an overwhelming torrent of rock and ash. What was an unimaginable nightmare for the two cities' inhabitants, however, later became a boon to historical scholarship as the disaster meticulously preserved two separate instances of first-century Roman towns for future generations.

Small comfort for the ancient residents of the Bay of Naples, one would imagine—not many of us would be willing to cut our lives short to satisfy the curiosity of archaeologists two thousand years in the future. But then, it's generally acknowledged that living right next to a volcano does tend to shorten one's odds in the great casino of life.

What's rather less appreciated, however, is that uncovering the past can be just as random and unpredictable a process as burying it.

University of Cambridge archaeologist Andrew Wallace-Hadrill, longtime head of the Herculaneum Conservation Project and past Director of the British School at Rome, is quick to point out society's sometimes quixotic relationship to the past.

His book, *Herculaneum: Past and Future*, has an entire chapter on "The Politics of Archaeology" where he describes how the rediscovery of Herculaneum and Pompeii in the first half of the 18th century was a perfect propaganda fit for Charles Bourbon of Spain who was keen to establish his new Kingdom of The Two Sicilies as an integral spot on the Grand Tour as a focal point of global culture. Subsequent periods of languishing disinterest were punctuated by periodic resonances of archaeological and political agendas, featuring Italy's post-Risorgimento government and again during Mussolini's fascist regime.

But while the triumphant invocations of national heritage is an all-too-typical part of most government propaganda, Andrew intriguingly describes how in several cases throughout history the exact opposite happened, as the past was *deliberately* forgotten.

A good case in point is supplied by the relatively recent excavations at Pozzuoli, a 17th-century city at the north end of the Bay of Naples that was built on top of the abandoned old Roman town of Puteoli.

> *"Not surprisingly, the excavators found quite a lot of statues. Of course Puteoli was a major Roman city and naturally there were loads of statues.*
>
> *"But the odd thing that they spotted was that the statues had been deliberately abandoned there in the process of backfilling the site in order to build the new city on top. That is to say, the people who backfilled it **knew** that they were throwing away ancient statues.*
>
> *"And I was really struck by that, because then I thought, 'Ah. The interesting question is not just, Why do people excavate and look for the past? but, When do they **not want to find** the past?*
>
> *"And then I put that together with the well-known fact that, at the end of the 16th century, in the 1590s, a major architect called Dominico Fontana dug a big canal to bring water from the mountains behind through to the area of Torre Annunziata, which is just by Pompeii. And he sent his canal right through the ruins of Pompeii.*
>
> *"You know, constructing a canal is no minor engineering work. We can see the canal going right through the site with absolute clarity and it cuts a very impressive section through the southern part of the city. There is no way he didn't know that he was finding Pompeii. And yet, nothing was said about it.*

"That's in the same sort of time frame of people who actually bury ancient statues rather than dig them up. The obvious guess is in the times of the Inquisition you really don't want to find pagan antiquity. But the difficulty with that interpretation is that during the same period in Rome they were quite involved with finding pagan antiquity, like the Laocoön Group seen by Michelangelo.

"Maybe, in the south, in the Spanish-dominated south, they were more against paganism or what have you, but for whatever reason, they **found** Pompeii, they **found** Herculaneum, and they **didn't** want to know about it. And that, to me, is as fascinating as the people who **did** want to know about it.

"And suddenly, you see, you've got to explain **why** they want it. It's not obvious that people want to discover the past. They want to discover the past because it's useful to them."

All of which might lead you to naturally wonder whether or not, generally speaking, the past is useful to *us*.

The modern-day visitor to Herculaneum or Pompeii would certainly be tempted to think otherwise. The sites are generally acknowledged to be in a dangerous state of disarray, with expert voices consistently warning us that, without a well-coordinated national and international effort, we are running a serious risk of having these great archaeological treasures simply erode out from under us.

"I think it's deeply built into our picture of archaeology that it's somehow a way of rescuing the past, that you're saving the past by digging it up.

"Well, you're certainly saving it from oblivion in that you didn't know anything about it until you dug it up. But in terms of its own survival, the best place for archaeological remains to be is where they are: underground. There's nothing that preserves something so well as stable conditions of burial—on the whole, burial produces stability.

"You think that by digging it up you've saved it, but you never dig up something that is capable of standing on its own two feet. You

> have to intervene at once in order to ensure that it doesn't crumble under your eyes.
>
> "And so, in a very interesting way, the process of excavation is a process of conservation and restoration: you must do something with it."

Reasonable enough, you might be tempted to agree. But then what, exactly, *should* we be doing?

Well, as you might expect, the situation at Pompeii and Herculaneum is greatly complicated by several overlapping layers of government bureaucracy along with a welter of additional international interests.

Through it all, however, Andrew holds out several reasons for optimism, maintaining that the basic road map to begin effecting real positive change is actually quite straightforward.

> "It's actually remarkably simple: Get the roofs right and you can save the rest of the site. Leaking roofs cause more problems than anything else. Most of the problems of conservation of decorated surfaces start with problems of damp. Sort out the problems of damp. It's not all that difficult. You get the roofs right, you get the drains right, and the damp goes away. And **then** you can send in the people to conserve the wall paintings, but so long as the walls are damp you're wasting your money on conservators. You've got to get the damp problem sorted out—and those damp problems can be fixed right across Pompeii."

The Bay of Naples has certainly seen its share of horrors in the past. But the future, perhaps, might still be quite bright.

The Conversation

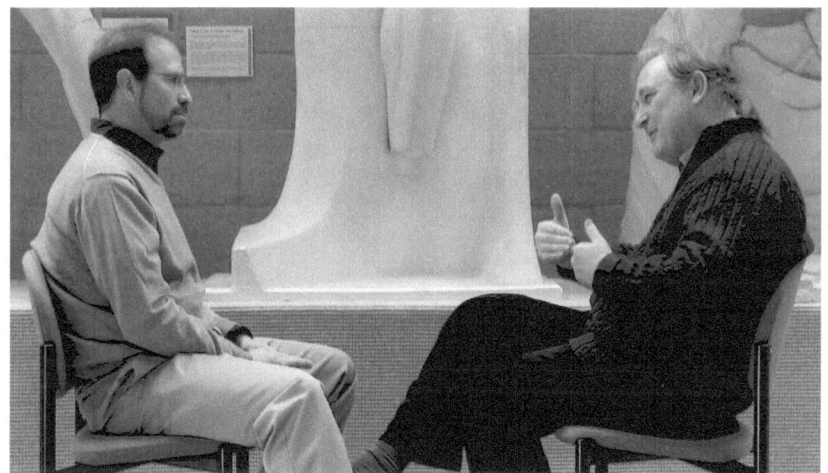

I. What We Know
History and geology

HB: Perhaps I could ask you to start us off by providing some general historical context about the history of the excavations at Herculaneum.

AWH: Well, the real excavation of Herculaneum happens under the Spanish regime of Charles Bourbon (King of Naples and Sicily from 1734-1759). That's the great period of excavation. He took a very strong personal interest in it.

And they just explored everywhere. They started at the theatre but it's a mining principle: you go down and then you go laterally, and they riddled the site with their tunnels—absolutely riddled it. And every now and again they would just hit something really spectacular.

They hit the Villa of Papyri at around 1750. Suddenly—boom!—statues are coming out. I think it's a wonderful historical irony that Charles Bourbon was the inheritor of the biggest collection of ancient statues in Italy: the Farnese collection.

In his mind, the obvious thing was, *Let's find statues!* And he was so lucky because, well, where do you find statues? You find them in the theatre, you find them in the public buildings and you find them in very big villas with gardens. And he manages to hit all of them.

Imagine hitting a villa, if we did it today, with a hundred statues of quality. It's the most incredible find imaginable. And then, as if that wasn't enough, a unique collection of carbonized papyri. It was the most unbelievable bit of luck.

Given how truly amazing that find is, the odd thing is that people later lost interest in Herculaneum. And there I blame the famous German art historian and archaeologist Johan Joachim Winckelmann, who attacked the excavations.

HB: The way they were being done.

AWH: Yes.

HB: This was after Charles had gone back to Spain, right?

AWH: Yes. Charles had gone back to Spain in 1759 to become King Charles III, leaving his son Ferdinand to succeed him as King of Naples. But Ferdinand is only eight years old when he starts—it's an incredibly delicate regime.

And Bernardo Tannucci, Ferdinand's prime minister, is trying to hang onto things when this damn German publishes this blast against Herculaneum. And the next thing you find is that they've shifted their interest to Pompeii, about which Winckelmann had very little to say because there was nothing to see when he visited. So Herculaneum sort of goes off the radar in a really interesting way; and yet they had only just begun to discover these amazing things.

HB: I'd like to talk a little bit about your background and how you became involved with Herculaneum and Pompeii, but first I'd like to highlight a few misconceptions. Reading your book, *Herculaneum: Past and Present*, was a particularly stimulating experience for me because so many of my preconceived notions of what Herculaneum I thought the site to be were shown to be false.

For one thing, when I thought of Herculaneum, almost the only thing that I thought was noteworthy was the Villa of Papyri. All I could think about was, *We know that so much of ancient literature was lost and this could be a place where there's a lot more that we can find, since it hasn't been fully explored yet.*

Of course I still feel enormous excitement at the prospect of being able to find lost manuscripts, but I've also learned through your book that there are also so many other things there that are extremely captivating.

AWH: I think that's exactly what I want to say. The Villa has still a lot to offer, and all the work done recently on the Villa has come up with some really interesting results. But it isn't just papyri that you can get out of Herculaneum.

I myself am particularly interested in the documentary wooden tablets—legal documents, where you have the document in triplicate all tied together, inscribed inside and with an ink version on the outside. So far we've found, I think, eight different bundles of these at Herculaneum. And it's absolutely certain that if you do more excavation you will find more of them. They're incredibly hard to read, but they're much easier to read than the papyri because at least they were flat, not all rolled up.

The papyri are an extraordinary challenge to read, while the level of reward you get out of reading these legal documents—to me as a Roman historian—is much, much higher than what we've got out of the papyri. Not that Greek philosophy is of no interest—of course it's fascinating—but here you've got genuine, deep insights into how Roman business life worked, which is so precious.

Of course from the lawyers we have lots of written comments on how the law *ought* to be working: they give their own little case studies. But actually to see it in action on the ground—real people using the Roman legal system—you suddenly understand that the Roman legal system *matters* to ordinary people. They are absolutely engaged with it.

HB: I'd like to get a deeper understanding of what we have found, how we can interpret these results and the consequent aspects of Roman society that you've been able to penetrate in a deeper way through these finds, but first I'd like to dwell a bit longer on some of my misconceptions because I suspect that some other people might have them as well.

As I said, one misconception that I had was that the importance of Herculaneum effectively boiled down to just the Villa of Papyri. And that's clearly false.

Another misconception I had concerns what actually happened during the volcanic eruption. I don't know how I picked this up, exactly, but somehow I had this sense that Herculaneum was buried in a wave of mud after Vesuvius erupted.

And at the beginning of your book, you mention that the Cambridge archaeologist Charles Waldstein specifically puts this forward as an explanation of what happens. But it turns out to be completely wrong. And then you go on to talk about the clear and detailed interplay between archaeology and geology while highlighting what we now know actually happened during the eruption.

AWH: That's absolutely right. I mean, one thing that just awes me about engaging in the process of archaeological research is how you need to draw on all disciplines, particularly scientific disciplines. It's no good, for someone like me who is a historian by training, to try to understand how volcanic eruption works. You need a volcanologist.

And, fascinatingly, volcanologists have been very engaged with this really well-preserved evidence of a past eruption. Since the early 1980s, our understanding of how the eruption actually happened, the precise dynamics, has been transformed.

Irritatingly, the idea that Herculaneum was overwhelmed with a mud flow remains so ingrained in the literature. Nowadays, most Italians still refer to the rock that covers the site as *fango*—mud.

And, I always say, "Well, at least it's a two syllable word, fango, rather than the much more technical mouthful "consolidated pyroclastic flow".

And then, even more irritatingly perhaps, more technically the rock is called *tufo*, which in English is frequently mispronounced as "tufa", which is particularly problematic because tufa is actually the technical name for another completely different type of rock.

Meanwhile, Americans call tufo "tuff", but that's difficult for the Brits of course—we can't go around calling something "tuff"—so that's problematic too. All of this contributes, I think, to explain why *fango*—mud—sticks in the popular imagination.

HB: But it's completely wrong.

AWH: It's spectacularly wrong. Because what matters is not wetness and slowness, what matters is intense heat—these really hot gases swirling around, dense with ash. And without the heat you don't get the carbonization of organic materials.

Interestingly, you do also get waterlogging. One of the most exciting finds we ever made was down on the ancient shoreline where there was a whole heap of wood and the top layers were carbonized. The bottom layers, which were actually on the shore in the wetness of the sea, were waterlogged and not carbonized. So you do get waterlogging, but it is a completely different process from being overwhelmed in very hot gases and being carbonized.

HB: And these geological processes that you describe are quite different between Pompeii and Herculaneum, which in turn has such a wide impact on how things were preserved, or not, at the two sites. There is this wonderful interplay between geological science, archaeology and history.

It's quite the thing to sing the praises about interdisciplinarity these days: there's this sense of a biologist and a philosopher and an anthropologist in a room and wonderful things will necessarily start to happen. And most of the time it doesn't. But in your case it strikes me as quite different: there seems to be a necessary link across the very subject matter, which makes for a natural sort of interdisciplinarity.

AWH: I think we're very lucky to have had Haraldur Sigurdsson in our group, together with other colleagues. He was the person who really puzzled this out. And he is so clear in explaining the differences between what happened in Pompeii and Herculaneum that even a non-scientist can grasp it.

What you don't first expect is that the same volcanic eruption actually produces dramatically different effects within ten miles of each other. But then, of course, when you think about it a bit more in detail and you begin to appreciate the awesome process of material coming up from miles underground and exploding before coming back down again, it becomes quite apparent that it's a fantastically variegated process.

HB: And also how powerful it is. You mention this too—something else that shocked me when I stopped to think about it. I thought I had a pretty clear sense of what a volcano is: big eruption, lots of stuff coming out.

But when I read that this plume of smoke and ash was **27–33** kilometres high during the initial stages of the explosion of Vesuvius, I was simply astounded. 27-33 kilometres! You talk about the power producing this being roughly equivalent to atomic bombs exploding every three seconds or something like that. I mean, just the idea that this "pine tree of smoke and ash" as Pliny the Elder called it, was some 30 kilometres high. That's just remarkable.

AWH: It is absolutely awesome and very humbling. One of the things I do is a little calculation: if humans were trying to shift the amount of material that the volcano shifted in the course of 24 hours, how much effort would that take?

And the calculation that I came up with was that if you take the biggest truck on the market, which apparently takes 20 cubic metres of material, you would need **450,000,000** of them to shift that amount of material.

HB: In 24 hours.

AWH: In 24 hours. Nature moves on a very different scale from us. However much damage we inflict on this planet, it is nothing compared to natural phenomena.

I'm fascinated by Seneca, a famous philosopher and literary figure who was advisor to the Emperor Nero. One of the very interesting pieces he wrote—which is little read by classicists because it's a work on science—concerns his explanation for various natural phenomena, including earthquakes. He has a very clear picture of the awesome power of nature. And he draws this sort of perverse conclusion in saying, "*It's no good running away from an earthquake, because earthquakes can strike virtually anywhere*".

HB: This was after the big earthquake back in 63, or whatever, right?

AWH: Exactly. And he's right. In my lifetime there have been earthquakes up and down the Italian peninsula—it is very, very subject to earthquakes. And it's no good running away from Assisi to L'Aquila, if you're then going to find there's an earthquake in L'Aquila. So Seneca was right in saying that the danger of earthquakes was not confined to that volcanic area, because volcanic activity is spread up and down the Italian peninsula.

HB: But then you go on to say something else that I found particularly intriguing, which was that by examining the site carefully it is clear that there were significant long-term fluctuations in sea levels over a span of a century or two before the eruption. And anybody who is a modern-day geologist would recognize these changes in sea level as a very bad sign: it's an indicator that the Earth is buckling, or what have you, in preparation for a massive eruption.

So if you were a geologist in Seneca's day knowing what we know now, you might be very tempted to say something like: "*While it's true that bad things can happen everywhere, it seems that there might be something brewing in this particular neighbourhood that we should keep our eye on.*"

AWH: But one of the extraordinary things is our inability, our ongoing inability, to predict earthquakes and volcanic eruptions. Although there's an enormous scientific industry working on the problem, it's very hard to do so on human timescales. Italian civil protection has got a whole department of really high-quality scientists trying to work it out and they actually *imprisoned* scientists for their failure to predict the scale of the 2009 earthquake at L'Aquila, but there's no way that those scientists were being bad scientists. It's just unbelievably difficult to predict.

HB: Sadly, they didn't imprison Berlusconi for that, as it happens.

AWH: That would have been more satisfactory. But, he's the Teflon Don. He gets away with everything.

But I have to say that, for me, one of the most exciting moments of our project was watching our geologist colleague Aldo Cinque gradually tease out the implications of what had been happening down by the shore line, picking up all the corresponding bits of evidence that deepened our understanding of what happened.

"*Look, look,*" he'd say, "*There you have some sand under the building, but the sand is sitting on top of the traces of a quarry.*" More recently he has done a series of core samples, drilling down a ten-centimetre-wide core of about 30 metres or so to hit the ancient sea level.

So, gradually we're reconstructing a picture of the ancient coast line around Herculaneum. Another very interesting thing Aldo points out is that in the 18th century they made similar calculations on the basis of looking at wells and examining the stratigraphy. And they worked out a surprising amount correctly about the ancient shoreline from looking at wells. So the evidence is there, but it needs the experience and knowledge of a scientist to correctly interpret it.

Questions for Discussion:

1. Are you surprised at the extent of the influence of Johan Winckelmann's negative comments on the excavations at Herculaneum? Do similar levels of influence exist today on cultural matters?

2. Why do you think that Andrew is convinced that it is absolutely certain that if you do more excavation you will find more wooden tablets of legal documents?

3. Do you believe that there will come a time when scientists will be able to predict earthquakes and volcanic eruptions with much greater accuracy than they currently do?

II. Letting Sleeping Dogs Lie
Exploring historical motivations

HB: One last thing before I turn to more details about your involvement in Herculaneum and Pompeii. I was naively of the view, insofar as I had thought about it at all, that Herculaneum had been a completely lost city before it had been discovered in the 18th century.

But in *Herculaneum: Past and Future* you make several links between politics and archaeology, describing how we know of people who were exploring archaeological sites through what was dropped or left behind in the backfill of the tunnels that they dug. It seems, in fact, that over the ages there have been quite a few people who have discovered things and elected to keep silent about them for a number of political, cultural, religious or social reasons.

So the situation seems much less clear-cut than the naive notion that nobody knew about these places until they were first discovered. It might have been much more subtle than that: perhaps over the centuries quite a few people became aware of Herculaneum's existence and for some reason elected to say nothing about it at all.

AWH: Well, there are various strands to this argument, which is one I've put together over the course of time—after moments of revelation, so to speak. One really important moment was due to a discovery by my principal archaeological colleague on the project, Domenico Camardo, who is actually trained as a medieval archaeologist rather than a classical archaeologist.

He was clearing in one particular area and he became very excited, because he'd recognized some 13th-century pottery—it takes a trained medieval archaeologist to spot 13th-century pottery.

And he instantly saw the implications: he drew attention to other bits of evidence that people were aware—not so much that "Herculaneum" was there, but that there was an ancient city down below. And, in fact, when you look into the earlier literature, you find that there *are* antiquarians who do indeed speculate, "Herculaneum must be here."

But the second moment of revelation for me was when I was visiting Pozzuoli, which is on the north of the Bay of Naples. Pozzuoli suffered from dreadful earthquakes in 1980 and the whole historic centre had to be abandoned—it was in such terrible condition. And it remains so: this little area called Rione Terra is sealed off, it's a museum and not for people to live in.

There's a wonderful cathedral there, which is built in the remains of an ancient temple, and you can see the columns of the temple. In fact the earthquake actually helped us, because it "shook down" a lot of the Baroque decoration and made the Roman columns smile through.

So it's a really fascinating site; and after the earthquake it became possible to do excavations. And it emerged that there is a 17th-century city built on top of the abandoned and backfilled remains of the earlier medieval city that extended back to ancient times.

Not surprisingly, the excavators found quite a lot of statues: Puteoli was a major Roman city, so naturally there were loads of statues.

But the odd thing that they spotted was that the statues had been deliberately abandoned there in the process of backfilling the site in order to build the new city on top. That is to say, the people who backfilled it *knew* that they were throwing away ancient statues.

And I was really struck by that, because then I thought, *Ah. The interesting question isn't so much,* **Why do people excavate and look for the past?** *but, When do they* **not want to find** *the past?*

And then I put that together with the well-known fact that, at the end of the 16th century, in the 1590s, a major architect called Dominico Fontana dug a big canal to bring water from the mountains behind through to the area of Torre Annunziata, which is just by Pompeii. And he sent his canal right through the ruins of Pompeii.

HB: Hard to miss.

AWH: That's right. Constructing a canal is no minor engineering work. We can see the canal going right through the site with absolute clarity and it cuts a very impressive section through the southern part of the city. There is no way that he didn't know that he was finding Pompeii. And yet, nothing was said about it.

That's in the same sort of time frame of people who actually bury ancient statues rather than dig them up. The obvious guess is that in the times of the Inquisition you really don't want to find pagan antiquity. But the difficulty with that interpretation is that during the same period in Rome, they *were* finding pagan antiquity—like the Laocoön Group seen by Michelangelo.

Maybe, in the south, in the Spanish-dominated south, they were more against paganism or what have you, but for whatever reason, they *found* Pompeii, they *found* Herculaneum, and *didn't* want to know about it. And that to me is as fascinating as the people who did want to know about it.

And suddenly, you see, you've got to explain *why* they want it. It's not obvious that people want to discover the past. They want to discover the past because it's *useful* to them.

And then, to me, the other important argument is that the very same motivation that leads the Bourbon dynasty in the early 18th century to discover what was plainly discoverable feeds through to the modern tourist industry of today. That is to say, it's a magnet, you're creating a tourist magnet. Of course, it's a different kind of tourism back then compared to today.

HB: But the principles are the same.

AWH: Yes, the principles are absolutely the same. There's a continuity: part of the enormous fame and success of Pompeii lies in the fact that its reputation has gradually been built by this very slow process of discovery, with increasing levels of excitement and fiction built around it, until it enters not just the European imagination but the global imagination.

HB: There's this celebrated phrase, of course: *See Naples and die*. Perhaps it should have been *See Herculaneum and Pompeii and die*, but whatever—there's this sense that these are such immeasurably beautiful and important places that one's life cannot be complete unless one somehow partakes of them.

AWH: Yes. It is also the case that the Bay of Naples, in terms of natural beauty, is so extraordinarily stunning that even without the work of man it's worth going there to get the view. And that to me is an important thing about Herculaneum: it's a city that had this front row seat on the Bay of Naples with its spectacular view. And that's terribly important for how the site develops in the Roman period.

Questions for Discussion:

1. *Do you find Andrew's thesis convincing? What does he mean, exactly, by the "Spanish-dominated south"? Does the fact that the Laocoön Group was acquired by the Vatican make it harder to maintain? What other explanations might possibly explain this situation?*

2. *Does our society care more about the past than previous generations? Less? Does it depend on which place and time?*

III. Exploring Roman Society
Housing, slavery, citizenship and status

HB: So now, finally, to my long delayed question. How did you become involved in Herculaneum and Pompeii? And even before that, how did you become involved in archaeology?

AWH: The answer is actually a surprisingly simple one. It goes back to my teens, probably when I was about fifteen, when I started to get really interested in Roman history and I began to form the ambition to be a Roman historian.

My dad, who was a medieval historian, said *"Well, if you're interested in this stuff, I'd better take you to Italy"*. So we had a family holiday in Rome and Sorrento. For two weeks I had my first views of Rome, my first visits to Pompeii, Herculaneum, the museum in Naples, Paestum and so much else on the Bay of Naples. It made a deep impression on me.

I then returned as an undergraduate. I did a paper on Pompeian art as part of my undergraduate course. So those things became really important for me. They didn't become part of the focus of my research, however, until I had finished my doctorate. My doctorate was actually about Suetonius' *Lives of the Emperors.*

HB: Oh, really? Quite different, then.

AWH: Yes, a completely non-archaeological subject. But one of the conclusions I reached studying Suetonius is that what you get out of him is a picture, not just of the stories of individual emperors, but of Roman society and culture: how they fit in and affect the culture of their times. And that led me to want to write a book about Roman society and culture during that period. At that stage Pompeii and Herculaneum were already familiar to me, so I thought to myself, *Well, it would be really good to build in archaeological evidence.*

I started reading around what had been written and I was absolutely horrified. The literature was obsessed with Roman wall painting: the different styles of Roman wall painting, what precise dating each style had and so forth. There seemed to be no interest in the house as an archaeological unit, let alone a social unit. And here you've got this wonderful source that tells you not just about the elite—though it tells you about the elite too—but by definition it tells you something about the entire society.

You've got to have the entire society preserved in the archaeological remains of a city. And that's the very part that you're least confident that literature will get you into.

So I thought, *Let's do some serious research here.* I did lots of statistical analysis on what the differences are between the houses one can reasonably attribute to the elite compared to the others, going down the social scale.

And what I was enormously struck by was the continuity, that there is an imitation at lower levels of the social language. Here's a little example: one of the most beautiful villas just outside Pompeii at a place called Oplontis, has lovely little decorative birds on the corridor walls. And you can find exactly the same sort of birds in little shops and workshops in Pompeii—not so beautifully executed, but it's the same.

And I thought, *OK, you've actually got a continuity of culture in this society. You haven't got an enormous gap between an educated elite and the others who live in misery. There's a really important middle ground and there's a really important spectrum.*

And that was the subject of my first Pompeii and Herculaneum book, *Houses and Society in Pompeii and Herculaneum*. I was absolutely astonished how little work had been done on that at the time. Things have changed an enormous amount since then, I'm now completely out of date on the literature because it's gushing out.

So that's what got me into serious work on research—not just reading about Pompeii or simply visiting. But then, the next crucial step was my move to Rome. It was an extraordinary opportunity to be made Director of the British School at Rome. It required me to research in Italy. And the most obvious thing in the world was to develop projects in the places I had studied most. In terms of archaeological exploration I took it up a level, first with a project in Pompeii and then with a project in Herculaneum.

I'm deeply grateful for that opportunity of living in Italy, because unless you spend real time on these sites you can't get deep into them.

HB: How long were you there for?

AWH: Fourteen years.

HB: I'd like to get back to this idea of this continuum between different strata of society and houses in particular. In *Herculaneum: Past and Future* you mention not only an "intellectual continuum"—such as what you just referred to a moment ago in terms of the birds and what people might find beautiful to have on their walls or maybe otherwise interesting to think about—but also a sense of a *physical* continuum.

Nowadays we might naively imagine something like, *Well, there were rich people and there were poor people, and the rich people must have been in gated communities, as it were, like we have now.*

But because of their societal structures, because you had slaves and you had freed slaves and all of these people that were so integrally part of a wealthy person's abode, my understanding is that people of different classes weren't physically sealed off from each other at all.

AWH: That's absolutely right. I remember at an early stage of my research on Pompeii and Herculaneum I tried the very simple technique of measuring the plot sizes of these various different units and colouring them according to plot size. And what you get in a block of houses in Pompeii or Herculaneum is the full colour range: everything from the biggest to the smallest and everything in between. It's a very vivid picture.

I remember showing a slide of that in a talk to some school kids and during the question time, one kid who obviously came from a particularly comfortable background asked me, "*But did the Romans... were they **really** prepared to live cheek by jowl with so much poorer people?*"

And I blessed them for exposing their own social prejudices so exquisitely—I thought, *Thank you, you've really helped me here.* Because *that* is what is really so striking: that a Roman would have *never* asked me that question. Why doesn't a Roman even think that it might be odd to have much poorer people living in the same plot? And one answer is in the nature of Roman ownership.

You may, owning the block or a part of the block, own a little shop. And you may actually get someone who is a dependent in some sense—typically an ex-slave—to run that little shop for you. If you've got relationships of dependence that means within a household the rich, *of necessity*, live cheek by jowl with slaves, ex-slaves, and people like that. Then on the ground you find the same mixture. All this is utterly unlike our modern world, let alone a gated community.

Then as I pursued that issue further, I was very struck by how very much that segregation is a phenomenon of the industrial world. It's not really until the 19th century that this kind of physical segregation kicks in.

There's a really interesting study of New York that was looking at traces of houses from the 18th century and the 19th century, their pottery and so on, while comparing it to lists of where people lived. And it turns out that there's an enormous change that happens in New York as people move from a situation where they're living in the place of work to a situation where there are separate areas of shops and residential areas.

This also has enormous implications for gender differences. Suddenly the women, instead of being there in the place of work, are based in separate residential places with different kinds of pottery with which they're entertaining other women at tea. And you get this big sea change in society that results from the separation of place of work and place of residence.

So actually one way to look at things is that the Roman world is part—a distinctive part, but part—of an older world which we've most definitely lost the understanding of.

HB: There was this deep integration of place of work and place of residence—they were inextricably linked.

AWH: That was a very important part of the argument of my first book on Pompeii and Herculaneum, where I tried to show that you can't simply separate public and private. Public or external life necessarily enters into the private house because it's a place of work, but it's also a place of political work, of reception, of forming social ties and so on. And that again makes it so unimaginably different from how a modern house is contoured.

HB: There's also this key notion that one sees time and again throughout Herculaneum, which is the role of the freed slave. This was yet another thing I was completely unfamiliar with. I knew that there were slaves who were freed from time to time, and I had assumed that if one were a freed slave one was obviously on a better social footing than a slave, but there would always be this sense of discrimination, this inability to rise throughout the society and gain real wealth and so forth.

Not so, it seems, according to what you have written. There seems to be a particularly strong social role for freed slaves in Herculaneum, and in fact many of them seem to be very socially powerful and very wealthy. This came as a complete shock to me.

AWH: I think there are two big issues here: of number and of integration.

Number is still an enormous puzzle, because if we follow the evidence, the evidence of gravestones, the evidence of lists of names and so on, freedmen seem to form an improbably large portion of the population. It's almost as if people have given up having children and have slaves instead, reproducing through giving freedom to slaves. Now, evidently it can't be quite that much, but there *is* a sense in which slavery, in the family, substitutes for children. It's much easier to have fewer children if the work is going to be done by slaves together with having a trusting relationship with ex-slaves.

There's no doubt that a certain stain was always attached to slavery. An ex-slave was always an ex-slave, people didn't forget. And ex-slaves were excluded from certain areas of public life: they could never hold magistracies, for example. But they could certainly make money. And there's abundant evidence that they're deeply involved in business on the Bay of Naples.

And if you make a lot of money, of course you carry weight in a society. The interesting thing is how you deal with that dissonance between the wealth and the inability to participate fully in a politically-organized society.

You can't be a magistrate—we were talking earlier about the way that bundles of legal documents show the engagement of the population of a town in legal processes. Now, the people who give judgement, the magistrates, are a class apart, and the freedmen can never be part of that. So while you'll frequently find their names engaging in lawsuits, acting as witnesses and so forth, you'll never find them giving judgment. There is, then, something from which they're excluded—but there is at the same time the social power which wealth brings.

In my view, this is part of what the archaeological evidence is showing you: how they could use those things that *were* accessible to them—which are often the things that are archaeologically visible: after all, it's much easier to see a house with a beautiful marble floor than the fact that someone was a magistrate.

The old interpretation tended to be, *The moment you see a beautiful marble floor it must be a member of the elite, it must be a magistrate.* Well, not necessarily. The really interesting thing is that you can't tell, because the ex-slave who's made good has the same power to decorate a house.

HB: You also mentioned the College of the Augustales. This was a separate club, it seemed, and the majority of the members were ex-slaves, right?

AWH: That's correct. It's a phenomenon that is clearly connected with the cult of Augustus and what was called "the divine household"—the "*domus divina*"—not just Augustus but his wife and children and relatives are all part of a quasi-divine grouping that deserves cult status.

But at the same time Roman citizens did not worship other Roman citizens as if they were gods. Citizenship is all about some sort of equality: a citizen does not worship another citizen. That's the great paradox in it. But the people who *can* worship citizens are ex-slaves.

So it's not quite clear how, but it becomes institutionalized: you get these bodies of people who are typically ex-slaves—not exclusively, but typically—who are responsible for the cult of the *domus divina*.

To belong to that group is clearly a social privilege and one of the signs of that privilege is the order in which you receive your portion at a big public feast, which is typically given very hierarchically.

One of the ways of buying credit, political and social credit, in an ancient city was that you give a public feast. So, the Decurions, the members of the town council, they're the real elite, the magistrates and ex-magistrates, they get the best portions. But after them, the Augustales, the ex-slaves, they benefit from public feasts.

HB: These are the ones who have good marble patterns on their floor, presumably.

AWH: Yes, exactly! And then you get the plebs who get the smallest portions, if they get anything at all. You may have money handouts where there's the same sort of hierarchical distinctions. So it is evident that there were ways of giving social respectability to people who in theory could never be socially respectable.

And I guess a Roman would stop me at this point and say, "*Hang on a moment. We don't just classify people by whether or not they've* been slaves. *What we care about is moral qualities: whether or not you are a good person or a bad person is much more important than whether or not you are a slave or an ex-slave."* You'll find Seneca saying things like that.

So a good slave, who becomes a good ex-slave, is a better Roman than a bad freeborn person. Being Roman is all about virtue.

Questions for Discussion:

1. Might a future historian be able to determine the increasing levels of social inequality in our society by a careful examination of living quarters of rich and poor?

2. To what extent is it possible to judge the moral character of a slave? For an alternative perspective of how the ancient Romans equated freedom with social status, the reader is referred to Chapter 1 of **Quest for Freedom** *with intellectual historian and political philosopher* **Quentin Skinner**.

IV. Herculaneum vs. Pompeii
Different eyes on the past

HB: I'd like to compare Pompeii and Herculaneum a little bit, not only because you're an expert in both but also because you've written quite suggestively of a visual metaphor involving the two: that they are like two eyes, and to get a deeper understanding of Roman society at the time, you need to consider them both together.

Yet again I must admit to having had misconceptions about this, which I'm guessing some others might have had too.

Pompeii is, of course, a much bigger city than Herculaneum. And I had this sense that Herculaneum was a small town, a wealthy seaside resort inhabited by educated and well-behaved upper classes, whereas Pompeii was a place loaded with sex and violence for the teeming masses.

And you point out that it's true that there is much more sexually suggestive graffiti and evidence of gladiatorial games and all that in Pompeii, but that's not all. There was a certain type of political advertisement that one finds in Pompeii that one doesn't find in Herculaneum. And you also mention that the graffiti generally has a higher literary quality in Pompeii than in Herculaneum. So it's not true to say, "*The inhabitants of Herculaneum were the educated, cultivated, literate people as opposed to all those vulgar, tawdry masses who lived in Pompeii.*" That's a specious distinction, at best, it seems—if not just downright wrong.

AWH: One of the permanent difficulties in archaeology is understanding whether a contrast that you see is a real contrast or the result of the small sample that you have happened to have excavated.

Is Herculaneum *really* different from Pompeii or might we excavate a different Herculaneum which would make it much more like Pompeii?

You could say, *"Well, as it happens, the bit of Herculaneum we have excavated is the bit down towards the sea. And naturally, the rich wanted the houses with the sea views, and they dominate our impression of the town."* On the other hand, if you took away the great brothel from Pompeii, that picture of Pompeii as the city of sin would almost collapse on you. The percentage of sexual graffiti that is concentrated in that brothel is quite overwhelming.

Now, just suppose that Herculaneum had a brothel that is just off the edge of the excavations and we don't happen to have excavated it. Just because we haven't found a whole slew of obscene paintings and graffiti in Herculaneum doesn't mean that there was no brothel, no prostitution, and they were much more upmarket.

Jumping to such conclusions puts one on very shaky ground indeed—and there's already a big exception in Herculaneum, which is the suburban baths.

There's just one room in the suburban baths that has obscene graffiti in it. As it happens, it's a room that can no longer be accessed unless you crawl with great difficulty through a sort of window opening. But it has this wall that is completely covered in extremely explicit graffiti, recounting the adventures of a pair of slaves or ex-slaves in the Imperial Service who'd been down to Herculaneum and had participated in an orgy with a couple of girls. And so, suddenly, sex is back again because you've got that one little space.

So it's terribly dangerous, in my view, to generalize. Suppose you were to base your conclusions of Pompeii just on the excavations that ran along the walls of the city. You would find very grand houses there and you might well get the impression of a much more upmarket Pompeii. The great thing about Pompeii is that the excavations are so extensive that you've got an enormous range of stuff there.

So I say all that as a sort of caution: never assume because it isn't there *now* that it *wasn't* there in antiquity.

But all that being said, the sites *do* have a different feel. Again and again they seem to be not quite the same. A very interesting example is the decoration of the walls. It belongs to the same family, the stuff that's been done in Herculaneum, but it's terribly distinctive.

HB: How so, exactly?

AWH: One distinctive form was a blue background, with thin columns picked out in monochrome browns. Now that idiom of a field divided by architecture is very much the Pompeian idiom. But that way of using a blue or a black background, pretty flat background, and then these details picked out in monochrome, is very specific to Herculaneum.

Clearly they did things differently there—not necessarily because they were a different social class, but because they drew on a different set of workshops.

So to me that's why I like to think of that image of the two eyes that are quite close together to get the full picture. They're very similar to each other, Pompeii and Herculaneum, but they have slightly different perspectives. And the great danger with Pompeii is that you would simply take it as a universal model for a Roman town.

Well, just move ten miles around the bay and things are not exactly the same. In some respects they are, in some respects they aren't. And that, in itself, is already enormously valuable.

It's also true, I must say, that I've become plagued by people who want me to say that Herculaneum is better than Pompeii.

HB: You've been *plagued* by these people? Who's desperate to have you say this?

AWH: They want to egg me on to say it. And of course if I can assist some worthy cause I am happy to say, "*Herculaneum is much better than Pompeii*". But it isn't. The two are absolutely great.

Herculaneum gives you specific things much better than Pompeii. Pompeii gives you other things. If you want a picture of Roman public life, of a forum, of the amphitheatre, the world of trade, all these things you see better in Pompeii. So some things are better on one side and some things the other. But you need the two of them to supplement, reinforce, comment on the other.

HB: You also mention that there is a clear difference in the way the eruption buried the two towns, not only the extent to which they were buried—the four hundred and fifty million trucks and so forth—but also the actual geological material, the type of ash and rock. Perhaps most significantly, if I recall correctly, there is the structural difference whereby the second story of buildings is preserved in Herculaneum, while it isn't in Pompeii.

AWH: I have to say, having spent a long time working on Pompeii as well, one of the things that used to drive me crazy there was trying to understand the upper floors. You could see the evidence—you can see the bottom of a staircase going upstairs—you know that they've got an upper floor. You can see the drainpipe from the latrine upstairs coming down: you know it's there. But it's gone. Because, on the whole, Pompeii is preserved to 4–5 metres, whereas the depth of cover in Herculaneum is a minimum of 12 metres, with the greatest depth of up to 25 metres. And that's what enables second floors to survive.

And it's from Herculaneum that you can understand just how important those upper floors were. It gives a picture—to go back to a thing we were discussing earlier—of the complex relationship of what makes up a household: you can have tenants in a house, you can have the upper floors inhabited by completely different people. And because they're completely different people they need their own smart dining room and they need their own kitchen, and latrine, and so on.

You can actually *see* these things in Herculaneum; you have to posit them in Pompeii. At Pompeii, we know there's something going on but we can't quite understand how important it was. It comes back into focus in Herculaneum, and that's really valuable.

Questions for Discussion:

1. What sort of people do you think would be determined to egg Andrew on to claim that Herculaneum is superior to Pompeii and why? Has this chapter made you reconsider your own beliefs about the difference between the two towns?

2. If we were to discover another buried ancient Roman city how might that change our understanding further? At what point do you think we could be confident that we "understand" Roman society?

V. The Future of the Past

Excavation, preservation and spending effectively

HB: There are two more topics I'd like to discuss. The first is the importance of restoration along with excavation.

Every so often, I'd notice an announcement in the newspaper that the excavations at Herculaneum have stopped. And I'd become almost indignant, thinking to myself, *Come on, get your act together! What's stopping you people?* Because—as I mentioned earlier—I was really focused on this whole business of finding all those lost manuscripts that might be lurking there, hidden just beneath the surface, waiting for to be discovered.

But in *Herculaneum: Past and Future*, you stress the importance of responsible excavation, the importance of preserving the remains both for ourselves and future generations. You emphasize this point that once we excavate something, once we dig it up, it becomes exposed to the elements; and we are, from that moment on, seriously jeopardizing its ability to be able to last. And we must take that into very serious consideration before we even begin.

AWH: I think it is deeply built into our picture of archaeology that there's somehow a way of rescuing the past, that you're saving the past by digging it up.

And you're certainly saving it from oblivion in that you didn't know anything about it until you dug it up. But in terms of its own survival, the best place for archaeological remains to be is where they are: underground. There's nothing that preserves something so well as stable conditions of burial. You don't want the conditions to change too much, but on the whole burial produces stability.

You think that by digging it up you've saved it, but you never dig up something that is capable of standing on its own two feet. You have to intervene *at once* in order to ensure that it doesn't crumble under your eyes.

So in a very interesting way, the process of excavation is a process of conservation and restoration: you must do something with it. And one of the things we know by looking at detail at the site of Herculaneum, was that the principal excavator, Amedeo Maiuri, was an absolutely brilliant restorer—a brilliant and, by modern standards, somewhat unprincipled restorer. An extraordinary amount of what looks like a vividly surviving ancient house is Maiuri's wonderful reconstruction of an ancient house.

The complexity of that relationship between the real ancient remains—between reconstruction of what he could be absolutely confident was missing (because it's more of the same)—and guesswork, or just the most convenient way to preserve it—especially at the upper levels—is so complex.

The trained archaeologist gets an eye for it quite rapidly, and is able to say, "Ah, yes: **that's** Maiuri; **that's** Rome".

We reckoned it was something like 50% of the site was built by Maiuri rather than by the Romans. So the moment you realize that excavation goes with very considerable modern intervention, the more important it becomes to understand, and to record, what is actually Roman. But you've also created a need to continuously sustain those things that you have elaborately rebuilt.

So if I've got one message, it is that archaeology *must be* intimately connected with conservation, and that conservation *is* archaeology: that by doing work to preserve the remains of the past, you continually discover new things about it.

HB: But how do we make sure that this is being done, or at least being done sufficiently well? I read something in the newspaper not too long ago that Pompeii is falling apart: it's a disaster, it's in a state of crisis. On an organizational level, what do we do to make sure that we're doing things better?

Let me ask a very specific question: if you were King of the World, and you had the opportunity to organize things in whatever manner you saw fit, what would you do differently?

AWH: What would I do differently? I would necessarily find myself dismantling and rebuilding the whole system by which antiquities are looked after in Italy. Now, I speak with the most profound respect for my colleagues—some of my closest friends are the people who are responsible for looking after these sites. But it is through their eyes that I see that they feel themselves trapped in a system with a set of regulations and laws that render what they're trying to do almost impossible to deliver: it is heartbreakingly difficult to do quite simple, necessary things on site.

To take but one example, one of the principal problems is the set of laws that govern public works. Now, for absolutely proper reasons the Italian state has legislated in such a way that you can't spend public money without having open competition for the contracts, and that you have some obligation to give the contract to the lowest qualified bidder.

But that system has turned into an utter nightmare, whereby you get eighty people bidding for a contract. How do the archaeologists responsible for the site distinguish between those building firms that are contaminated by the Camorra, the local mafia, and those which are not?

How do you distinguish between those that are honest and those that are corrupt? There are so many opportunities in any building job for making money by *not* supplying what was specified but by supplying a cheaper version of what was specified.

The impact of the devastating 2009 earthquake in L'Aquila was made much worse by the fact that student buildings had been constructed with sea sand in the concrete. Sea sand is cheaper than builder's sand and inescapably has salt in it which leads to the collapse of a modern building. Appalling things sometimes happen in construction—not just in Pompeii and Herculaneum and not just in Italy—builders take shortcuts everywhere.

HB: But presumably when it comes to archaeological sites, it's even harder to have guarantees of sufficient professionalism. You mention sea sand and various corners being cut, I can imagine the potential number of shortcuts would multiply by orders of magnitude when you're talking about very abstruse, abstract, conditions for ensuring preservation that require a high degree of technical sophistication.

How can you have the assurance that a professional partner is not trying to cut corners, that he is going to pay sufficient attention to all of these details that require so much refinement and so much awareness?

AWH: The answer to that is that it's all perfectly possible, as we have demonstrated in Herculaneum. The great advantage we have there is being a *private* entity, because private entities are not governed by the laws that govern the spending of state money.

If you've got the right people—and a part of the essential recipe has been to have a team of experts in the right disciplines—to select the building firms, those who are looking out for competence not for the cheapest bid, then that's an essential beginning.

And if you *first* draw up high quality specifications for the job, *then* select high quality firms and *then* supervise them in detail as they execute the work, it is perfectly possible to do these things well.

What is so difficult is for the Italian state, operating under its public works legislation, to do that. And the paradox of our project has been the fact that Italian state itself has encouraged a private partner to do what it knows it has tremendous difficulty in delivering.

I think one answer is that you've got to produce new legislation that is quite specific to the public works on an archaeological site, specifically Pompeii and Herculaneum: you've got to free up the red tape that makes it so difficult to select the best firms, and you've got to concentrate on having the right expertise to draw up the right specifications, to select the right people, and to supervise the project. It's perfectly doable.

The big challenge for Pompeii at the moment is that with this enormous grant—well, it's not so big as it seems, but a hundred million euros to be spent over the course of three years does seem like a lot of money—that's a very tight time frame for changing your system completely while spending the money well.

And we all know—and they admit it themselves—that they're going to be very, very hard-pressed to spend that money in time in an effective manner.

HB: Where does this grant come from, exactly?

AWH: It comes from the European Union.

HB: So it's intergovernmental.

AWH: Exactly. And the problem will not be solved in three years. I would say that it would take a minimum of twenty years of sustained work on the site of Pompeii to reverse the enormous decline. But the ray of hope comes from the fact that Italy was not always like this.

Back in the days of fascism, and back in the days of post-war Italy, Amedeo Maiuri found it possible to run his site with a group of very skilled workmen and do work pretty efficiently. I say "pretty efficiently" because we do find that sometimes the concrete ceilings he poured were underspecified, badly constructed and so on. So it's true that bad things happened even then.

But on the whole, if you go back to the early 1960s when he retired, the sites were in pretty good condition. And it's a very recent phenomenon, and in some ways it's a litmus test of a broader malaise in Italian politics, for which we use Berlusconi as the symbol. We all know that there are problems there, we all know that Italian politics is shot through with corruption and torn between the reality of corruption and legislation that's trying to control the corruption but instead of controlling it actually enables it. So at the highest level there are big political problems to solve in Italy.

Naturally, I can't set about solving the big political problems in Italy, but at least I can show what specifically needs doing on-site—and it's not rocket science, as they say. It's actually remarkably simple, the recipes for ordinary maintenance for intervention. I frequently say, "*Get the roofs right and you can save the rest of the site*".

Leaking roofs cause more problems than anything else. There's also the problem of *rising* damp as well as damp coming down, but most of the problems of conservation of decorated surfaces start with problems of damp. Sort out the problems of damp.

It's not all that difficult: you get the roofs right, you get the drains right, and the damp goes away. And *then* you can send in the people to conserve the wall paintings, but so long as the walls are damp you're wasting your money on conservators. You've got to get the damp problem sorted out—and those damp problems can be fixed right across Pompeii.

HB: So let's suppose we do that. Indulge me for a moment: we get the roofs right, we get the drains fixed and walls sorted out. And let's suppose—even more happily—we've reformed the Italian government to a large extent.

And we have a steady flow of NGO involvement as well, resulting in a perpetual flow of funding so it's not just one large announcement or a series of large announcements but there is a sustained series of resources that are dedicated to enabling the site to be preserved going forwards.

Now, my understanding is that something like, only half of Herculaneum, or perhaps a quarter of Herculaneum, has been fully explored and there are sites in Herculaneum and Pompeii, many sites, which obviously people would like to move forward exploring. On the other hand, there are people living in the area, who are living on top of these sites.

So in this happy world where we've been able to fix all of our preservation issues up until now, what else do we need to do going forwards? Is there a possibility of doing more excavations? *Should* we be doing more excavations? What would you do next?

AWH: Even we, in the course of our conservation projects, have been doing excavations. In order to drain the ancient shoreline, we had to complete the excavation of the ancient shoreline. It had been dug down to a convenient level, but not deep enough to drain it. We knew that in order to insert a system of drains, we had to complete the excavation, take it down to bedrock, and record it. Only then are you morally entitled to put something on top of it. And in that process of excavation we found the first example of a wooden roof ever excavated from the Roman world—a wonderful, wonderful thing. So we have been doing new excavations *in order to save the site*.

The site has very ragged edges. On one side there's a sort of great curve and a wall of *tufo* ("tuff"), a wall of rock. But on the other two sides it's just—well, they stopped digging where they stopped digging and you see buildings just disappearing into the edge of the excavation.

One reason, one *conservation* reason, for doing more excavation is that it's no good leaving a building sticking half in and half out of the side of an excavation. The problem is, you can't keep going on that basis: then you have to excavate the whole city. But of course you can find more sensible ways. So, tidying up the edge of the site is a remaining big challenge that has the potential for an enormous amount of discovery.

There's also the potential to find new ways of excavating and presenting things to the public. One possible approach is to go back to the 18th century, to go back to tunnelling. They found out so much about the site by tunnelling. Do we have to expose the site completely to the air, particularly in areas where there are modern houses built on top? Or could one simply enlarge tunnels, and instead of backfilling them make them a visitor experience? The feedback we're getting suggests that it would be a magical visitor experience to be able to go down a tunnel and see bits of a Roman building still encased in the rock. So it's worth doing more excavation simply to simultaneously explore the site while investigating different ways of presenting the site to the public.

There's no total separation between, *Conservation work is **this** and it's good*, and *Excavation is **that** and it's bad*. No. To conserve we must excavate, and the excavation is going to produce new stuff.

In the case of the Villa of Papyri, everyone wants to know, *Will there be more excavation of the Villa of Papyri?*

Absolutely the first priority has to be to clean up the trench that's already been created. A big campaign was done just four or five years ago, and that revealed all sorts of things that had been missed in the very rough-and-ready excavation done with bulldozers back in the 90s.

For instance, these wonderful decorated ivory plaques were found—glorious new finds came out. The lower levels of the atrium of the Villa of Papyri are sitting right there accessible for excavation; and there's a very strong reason for excavating them, which is that currently water, which passes through the rock at all sorts of levels, is visibly cascading through the lower levels of the building. So there is some urgency to tidy up excavations there and I actually strongly favour extending the excavations in the Villa of Papyri area.

But *not* in order to find more papyri. That seems to me very dangerous indeed, because you don't know *where* you're going to find more papyri, you don't know *if* you're going to find more papyri. Let's excavate what needs to be excavated in order to preserve it, and you might be rewarded by more papyri. Or there might be wooden tablets or little ivory plaques. We cannot tell what treasures will come out, but so far nobody has excavated on this site without exposing treasures.

HB: But in your view one of the things we will know for certain, if we do it right, is that we will have enhanced the opportunity to preserve the site, which is the whole point.

AWH: Yes. So I think there is an enormous scope for further archaeological work of a responsible sort that starts from the premise that archaeology and conservation must be interlocked in order to work.

HB: I know that you've had a close and longstanding relationship with the Packard Humanities Institute. Could you tell me a little bit more about that and the influence that they have had on both your work and the site more generally?

AWH: Well, this project simply would not have happened without the Packard Humanities Institute. The funding has been absolutely essential, but the importance goes far, far beyond funding. It's a very unusual kind of institute because David Packard himself takes such an intense personal interest in his projects. One of his principles has been that he will do a few projects and do them really seriously, invest real money in them, follow them with real interest. And his own personal contribution and interest has been of fundamental importance.

He's a classicist who has frequently visited the site. His observation on what the priorities should be, drive the project. For instance, he is deeply concerned that the visitor should be able to see the artifacts recovered from the site. He rightly understands that what you see in the museum in Naples is an integral part of your picture of Roman houses. And he's been very insistent throughout the project that we've got to get a site museum up and running.

For a number of years we explored the possibilities, and there actually is a physical building of a site museum, but it has never been open to the public because it was so badly constructed that it's never had approval to be opened. So we looked very seriously into whether or not we could make this building work.

HB: And can you?

AWH: The answer is no. It's such a series of disasters. I could keep you here for another hour telling you of the disasters of that particular building. At any rate David reached the conclusion that it would be better to start afresh. He has a vision of a museum that is also the visitors centre, the offices, the conservation centre—all the functions that you need on site, integrated.

It could be enormously important for the site, not just to provide a natural context for the objects to the visitors, all these wonderful domestic artifacts that are so essential—after all, you can't understand a bedroom without understanding the *things that come from a bedroom.*

But not only does it give the visitors back a missing part of their experience, it also makes the future financial viability of the site much more deliverable. If you route every visitor through a building, which is also a museum, which is also a restaurant, which is also a gift shop then you're bound to raise a great deal of additional revenue. This is a recipe that has been proved a million times in the States. Of course it could work.

HB: Indeed, but not just in the States. Think of all those shops in the underground passageway next to the Louvre.

Moreover, I'm guessing that those who are taking the time to go to Herculaneum and Pompeii are by and large very willing to support future excavations. They're not going there begrudgingly, and they're probably looking for mechanisms by which they can contribute to the future preservation of the site.

AWH: I'm sure you're right, because people often ask me, "*How can we help?*"

And the biggest obstacle to people helping is that no one wants to pour money down a black hole. If you know that something dreadful is going to be done with it, if you despair over the capacity of Italy to look after its own heritage, well, why should you contribute?

The real act of courage by the Packard Humanities Institute is that, confronted with clear evidence of maladministration and failure to look after the site, they have nonetheless invested substantial amounts of money in making it a site that can be looked after.

HB: Well, they're doing things in a different way. They're obviously not looking at transferring resources to the Italian government and getting out of the way. They're aiming to do something different in parallel to what it is currently being done.

AWH: Absolutely. There is a very distinctive American approach that is underlying all this. The institution that delivers this project is a British institution, the British School at Rome, of which I was Director for many years. And in many ways we see things incredibly closely to how America sees things. But nevertheless the initiative, the new ideas, typically come from the US; and California is a great place for new ideas to come from.

So I think that this private intervention is not simply "filling up a hole in the funding". It's providing funding that can be spent flexibly, precisely because it's not in the straitjacket of Italian public spending. It's funding that comes with a richness of ideas for the future potential of the site that really *is* transforming what is happening there.

HB: Notwithstanding the way that they pronounce "tuff".

AWH: Yes. Tough luck for those who find that a problem.

HB: Thank you very much, Andrew. It's been a pleasure chatting with you.

AWH: Thank you Howard. The pleasure is mine.

Questions for Discussion:

1. To what extent might the European Union be well-placed to impose appropriate conditions for substantial site improvement along the lines of a private foundation?

2. Are there also disadvantages associated with the level of influence that private foundations have on archaeological sites? If so, how might those be minimized?

3. How, if at all, has this book changed your perspective on Herculaneum, Pompeii and/or archaeology in general?

Continuing the Conversation

Readers are encouraged to read Andrew's book, *Herculaneum: Past and Future*, which formed the basis of this conversation and goes into considerable additional detail about many of the issues discussed.

Embracing Complexity

A conversation with David Cannadine

Introduction
Imposing Order

Physicists love laws. Not in the way that you might naively think, perhaps: that the universe should be littered with injunctions left, right and centre. No, to a physicist, the ultimate sort of laws should be as broad and all-encompassing as possible, with the fewest possible exceptions.

We're used to three, as it happens (so much so that when four laws of thermodynamics were discovered, we decided to rename the first one the "Zeroth Law" so that we wouldn't have to formally enunciate a fourth), but deep down, we'd all prefer just one really big one that applies to everything imaginable: the so-called "theory of everything" that can be written on a T-shirt or something.

That's why Isaac Newton, with his Universal Law of Gravitation that applied to everything in the known universe, from apples to planets, became such a poster-boy to physicists for generations ever after, despite his other rather insalubrious character traits (pettiness, vindictiveness and a general incapacity to enjoy the company of his fellow humans).

And that's why Albert Einstein, with his General Theory of Relativity that managed to fundamentally supplant Newton's framework while still ensuring the same breathtaking universality, is ensconced in our pantheon of heroes as well.

The fact that Einstein managed to do all of that while also evincing warmth, humanity and a love of the violin was an added bonus, but for a physicist it wasn't really the main thing. What really mattered was his transcendent ability to impose order on an otherwise chaotic and incoherent world filled with seeming arbitrariness and inexplicability.

In short, then, the business of physics is to try to uncover the guiding laws of nature, and the truly great physicists are the ones who actually manage to do so.

When it comes to history and historians, however, it's not quite so straightforward.

David Cannadine, for example, the Dodge Professor of History at Princeton University and one of history's most accomplished and well-recognized practitioners, takes a rather different approach to the role of both history and historians.

> *"When politicians and pundits and false profits stand up and say to us, 'The world is very simple, and I will tell you how simple it is and all we need to do to fix it,' it seems to me that it's constantly the job of the historian to say in reply, 'No, the world is very complicated; and you disregard that complication, not only at your peril but probably at ours as well.'"*

It's not that some historians haven't tried to find "laws of history", of course. Indeed, for a long time that was certainly the vogue among many of the field's practitioners, influenced by a spectrum of thinkers from Hegel to Marx, Max Weber to Arnold J. Toynbee.

Over time, all of those interpretations proved to be incorrect, or at least severely limited. All were recognized as offering a certain degree of explanatory power for some historical events, but none were the sort of comprehensive explanations of the past in the way that their original authors had intended.

But historians kept trying. Next came a focus on examining specific aspects of human identity as the driving force of historical circumstances: religion, or nationalism, class or gender, race or "civilization".

Over time, theories and interpretations multiplied, with each school demanding that its particular aspect of human identity—race, say, or gender—represented nothing less than **the** way to correctly interpret past events.

At the very least, the one thing that could be safely concluded is that they can't ***all*** be pre-eminent causal factors in driving historical events, a point that David took as the clear starting point for his book, *The Undivided Past: Humanity Beyond Our Differences*, where he methodically examines six identities side by side—religion, nation, class, gender, race and civilization—to try to see what claims were made on behalf of each.

> *"It turned out that each of them made totalizing claims for the pre-eminence of this one single identity of the conflicts arising out of those identities and of that as being the motive power that drove the historical process forward. So, for example, one hears, 'Religion is the most important identity which divides people and drives the historical process forward,' together with similar claims made for each of the other five. Self-evidently, they couldn't all be right.*
>
> *"My own sense was that probably **none** of them were right in those extravagant claims that they made, even though for most of us of course it's the case that, since we are people of multiple identities—having a religion, carrying a passport, having some sort of social- and occupational-determined identity, having a certain sort of skin colour, a certain gender, and maybe even signing up to a civilization—these are all often significant elements of our identities. But to elevate the claim of any single one of those above all others to be the most important thing about individual identity, collective behaviour, and the antagonistic processes which are assumed to drive the historical process forward seems to me to be a grotesque over-simplification. And part of the purpose of the book was just to lay all that out."*

But David's motivations weren't simply limited to pointing out logical contradictions and historical hubris among his colleagues. There's a wealth of growing scholarship that indicates that, in focusing so strongly on identities and group conflict, we've overlooked key aspects of the historical record.

"I wanted to draw out a lot of historical work—quite a lot of it rather recent historical work— which has explored, in different contexts and with reference to different categories, the sort of conversations across the boundaries of identity, which historians are becoming increasingly aware have occurred.

"For instance, in an earlier time it was commonplace to present the period of religious wars from the Reformation through to the end of the Thirty Years' War as a time of constant religious confrontation between Protestants and Catholics. What a lot of the recent work has shown is the extraordinary way in which, if you go down from the level of theological disputation or princes fighting each other in the name of one religion rather than another religion, and look at the way people, on the whole, were living out their lives, it wasn't on the basis of those antagonisms at all.

"There were households in which the servants might be of a different religious faith from the people who employed them. The churches were used for a Catholic service and then for a Protestant service. There was a whole variety of interconnections in ways that previously we hadn't understood as much as I think we now do.

"And, therefore, one of the things that the book tried to do is to report on the way in which historians—some historians, not all—have recently begun to see that the history of humanity is about the history of conversations and dialogue as much as it's about the history of antagonism and war."

So no historical "theory of everything", then, no pithy law that we can stick on our coffee mugs that sums up all human motivations and subsequent behaviour.

Except, perhaps, that there is no such law. Which is definitely a form of progress as well.

The Conversation

I. Finding One's Historical Feet
Merging subjective and objective

HB: Let's start at the beginning—that is to say, your beginning: how you became motivated and interested in history and becoming a historian. Was this something that had formed for you from a very early age? Were you passionate about history when you were a small child? How did it begin for you?

DC: It is a very good question; and, of course, it's one that I've asked myself a lot. As I get older, I increasingly wonder how I ever got to be doing what I've been lucky enough to do—that's to say, to persuade people for the best part of 40 years to pay me money to read and write books, which is an astonishingly privileged form of existence, really, for which I'm hugely grateful.

But to answer your question as best as I can: I was born in 1950 on the Western side of Birmingham. My mother's family came from what in those days used to be called the "Black Country", which was an area West of Birmingham devoted to industrial production. The Birmingham and the "Black Country" that I grew up in the 1950s was still, as I can now see and perhaps even understood at the time, in many ways recognizably a kind of 19th-century Victorian world. The changes in the southeast of England in the 1920s and 1930s, the Hoover factories and the arterial roads, had rather passed it by. I think I was always conscious of growing up in a world where there were a lot of things that were old, even though the 19th century wasn't old in the sense that Salisbury Cathedral would be thought to be old.

I was also struck by the fact that there seemed to be this rather close relationship between the countryside and the town. I lived on the western edge of Birmingham where these two things connected.

In particular, heading from where I lived into Birmingham, there was this very beautiful suburb where rich people (as it seemed to me at the time) lived, called Edgbaston. The land there was owned by an aristocratic family, who then leased out the plots for houses to be built (most of them had been built in the 19th century) on which middle-class and working-class people lived.

I was intrigued by that connection and I wrote about that in the school magazine when I was only twelve or thirteen. So, I had this curious sense of the 19th century being very close to where I was living and growing up. It was the world, in some ways, that I inhabited. I also had this quite complicated sense that the relations between different social groupings might turn out to be at least as much collaborative as, perhaps, adversarial. Now I'm probably over-doing that in retrospect, overdetermining it all.

HB: Well, you are an academic, after all.

DC: Yes, I am an academic; we're probably not very good on motivation, least of all on our own. But those were certainly some of the influences on me as a boy growing up in the 1950s and 1960s. In so far as there's a kind of central area of interest that is still my main preoccupation—though I've written more broadly on lots of other things—I suppose, to some degree, it is 19th and 20th century Britain.

That's really how it started. My father bought me lots of volumes of the *Pelican History of England*, as it then was, and I thought those were rather wonderful. I read those very avidly. I did read a lot; I was a very bookish child, I suppose. Somehow history became a subject for me of enormous fascination, and I was lucky enough to be growing up when a whole range of writers—Eric Hobsbawm, Asa Briggs, J. H. Plumb, Alan Bullock, A. J. P. Taylor, Owen Chadwick—were all producing books of major historical significance which also reached a broad reading public, of whom I was increasingly one. It was a rather marvellous time to be growing up, because ever year—or, indeed, every other month—there was a book by one of them coming out which was just hugely interesting to read. Asa Briggs, in particular, was a major early influence because he wrote this wonderful history of Birmingham, and ever after that's always been a book that I wish I'd had the chance to write when he had, which was when he was very young.

So, in general, I suppose it's a kind of mixture of things. I went to read history at university, because by then it was pretty clear that's what I wanted to do. I always remember going to what was then called "Careers Service" in my third and final year at Cambridge to get some advice.

I told them that I'd thought about the civil service, but I didn't really think that was for me. I'd thought about applying for scholarships to America and I thought that was a very good idea, helping me to become a research student and then a professional historian.

And the man said to me, *"David, I've been thinking about you, and I don't think the civil service is really quite your scene. I think perhaps you ought to consider applying for scholarships to America and then maybe you'd like to become a professional historian."* And I replied, "Thank you so much for that advice. I'd never thought of any of that."

HB: You mentioned this sense of history having passed one by, or at least a sense of modernity having passed one by to some extent, when you were growing up in Birmingham. But did you also have a sense that you were in a place that was imbued with the spirit of the Industrial Revolution? That you were close to the spirit of James Watt, an awareness of having been at a place that was at the heart of leading the world centuries earlier?

DC: It was certainly true that the physical creation of the world of Boulton and Watt and their contemporaries was still very much in evidence in the world in which I grew up. My mother's family, the "Black Country" side of the family, lived close to a whole network of canals and railway tracks which were still very much functioning in the late 1950s and early 1960s when I was growing up. The central area of Birmingham still looked exactly as it did in a very famous print that was done at Birmingham in the middle of the 1880s. It was this area called Chamberlain Square—named after Joseph

Chamberlain—and in the middle was a memorial fountain that had been put up to him in the early 1880s.

There was the town hall opposite, designed by Joseph Hansom (as in Hansom cabs), put up in the 1830s. There was the great civic library, in which, later on, I worked as an undergraduate. There was the counselor house and art gallery, and there was Mason College, which formed the core of what later became Birmingham University. The streets were still cobbled and there were still some tramlines. The trams didn't run by then, but the tramlines were still there.

One certainly had a sense of living in a sort of Victorian world, not least because from the mid 1960s onwards, large parts of it were demolished in a deliberate attempt to move Birmingham into the future. The phrase "The new Birmingham" was the fashion back then: the beautiful 19th century library was demolished and so was Mason College. There was a considerable uproar about that: the conservationist got very exercised by it.

There was, then, this sense as I was growing up of an awareness of an old world in which I grew up, which had obviously once been a hugely vigorous world, but by now no longer was, not least because the zeitgeist of the 1960s was, *We have to get rid of all this Victorian stuff and start again*. I was lucky enough just to catch the tail end of this Victorian existence and then to live through the era of the 1960s, when the prevailing mode was, *This all has to go: we have to start again, and surely we can do better*—which I'm not sure, in the end, we have.

But that certainly gave me a strong sense that there is the world of **now** and **the future**, and it somehow isn't the same as the world of **then**, in which, fortunately enough, I'd actually grown up.

HB: In terms of your principal areas of professional historical research, you've written prolifically about the British aristocracy, Victorian England, the monarchy. You've written a great deal about British history in the 19th and 20th centuries. Drawing a rather straight line between what you've just said and some of the works that you've later produced, one might think that this general topic or theme was always something that was in your subconscious, that you were constantly thinking and ruminating over these things. But did it ever become a conscious and deliberate choice for you?

I say this thinking about a conversation that I had with John Elliott, when he mentioned two things: his sudden discovery of Spain from an undergraduate trip that he had taken, but also this sense that British history was very crowded, and there was an understanding that it would be very difficult to break through. Did you feel that as well? Did you also have a sense that British history was "crowded" and would therefore be particularly challenging professionally? Or did you simply move, unhesitatingly, into the subject area that interested you the most?

DC: Well, I probably didn't know as much about it when I started as I ought to have done, and had I known more I might have acted differently. John was likely far more attuned to what he ought to be doing and what the field was when he started, I suppose.

My sense when I started out—this was in 1972, when I graduated from Cambridge and then went to Oxford and Princeton as a graduate student—was that in the early 1970s it was actually possible to have read pretty well all the serious history on 19th-century Britain that had been written. Not only was it possible to be completely up to date with what was coming out, it was also possible to feel that there was a whole variety of areas that were still ripe for investigation—and even, perhaps, conquest.

I'm not sure that's true now. We're now talking forty years further on, and it's now impossible to keep up with the field. And if you're starting out now, it's certainly impossible to have a mastery of it in the way that I was able to do when it was a much smaller field. Certainly, when I dived in in 1972—and I dived in, in part, to a subject that had a very considerable initial local inflection about the aristocracy as urban real-estate developers—it was possible to take the view that almost no work had been done on that at all. There was a whole area of urban history, social history, architectural history and cultural history about aristocrats with considerable fortunes who had made their fortunes (or, at least, large parts of them) not from owning broad-acred agricultural land and getting rent, but from doing a whole variety of other things of which urban real estate was one, investing in railways was another, owning coalmines was another and owning docks and harbors was yet another.

That was a largely unexplored field when I started off. There had almost been nothing written on exactly that combination of questions, and so there were huge areas where I was probably the first person to look at the archives. And when I wrote my first book (*Lords and Landlords: The Aristocracy and the Towns, 1774-1967*), there was a sense in which I was kind of opening up a subject, which other people have taken up since. I think it's developed very interestingly.

So while it is true that there was quite a lot written on some aspects of 19th-century Britain, especially the high politics, there were whole areas to do with economic history, social history, cultural history, and we would now say gender history, which hadn't been looked at all. It was still, actually, then—in a way that is much less so now—a fairly open field.

Questions for Discussion:

1. Do you think that historians or born or made?

2. In this chapter David highlights the many professional historians who influenced him during his youth. Do you think that today's professional historians have as much impact on the general public as those of earlier generations?

II. The Art of Biography
Trevelyan, Mellon, George V and more

HB: When I look at your work, I can certainly see many concrete examples of what you've been mentioning: *The Decline and Fall of the British Aristocracy*, *Ornamentalism*—general assessments both of how the British perceive their world in the 19th and 20th centuries and how they were perceived externally. All of that makes sense to me. But then, there's this biography of the American tycoon Andrew Mellon (*Mellon: An American Life*). Where did that come from? How did that happen?

DC: How did that happen? Well, it happened in the following way. At the time that I was asked to write it I was a professor of history at Columbia University. I taught in New York from 1988 to 1998, which gave me a kind of distance on British history that I've always found to be rather stimulating.

In any event, as a result of that, my wife Linda (Linda Colley, also a Princeton University historian) and I spent the summers back in Britain, because there was British history to work on. One Friday evening, the telephone rang and someone said, *"This is the Andrew Mellon foundation in New York. We want you to write the life of Andrew Mellon."*

And I said, *"This is David Cannadine in Norfolk, England. You must have the wrong number."* To this day, I think there is some thwarted biographer somewhere else, probably in New York, waiting for the phone to ring. At any rate, that's literally how it happened.

But there is always more than one explanation for things. The explanations that I later uncovered behind that were the following.

When Andrew Mellon died in 1937, an account of his life was commissioned by his two children, Paul Mellon and Ailsa Mellon Bruce, from a man called Burton Hendrick, who was a professional writer. Hendrick wrote the life, but he wrote it on such terms that the Mellons were paying him a fixed salary: he wouldn't get royalties from the book and they would decide whether the book should be published or not. In the end they decided, in the aftermath of Pearl Harbor and the world moving on from the times of Andrew Mellon, that they wouldn't have it published.

But Paul, who was Andrew's son and heir, ever after had it in mind that one of these days he would like to return to it. By the mid 1990s, which is when this phone call happened, he was in a sort of "ending up" mood. He had done his own autobiography, he'd republished the autobiography his grandfather (Andrew's father) had written, and he returned to the issue of whether the earlier unpublished biography by Hendrick should be updated and published, or whether they should start again. In the end, Paul and his advisors decided they would start again.

That's how they got to me. Now, exactly how many people actually said no before they got to me, I was never told. They claim none, but I'm not wholly sure of that.

I think they chose me, in particular, in the following way. At the time that I was teaching at Columbia, my wife, Linda, was teaching at Yale. Yale was, of course, Paul Mellon's university, and one of Paul's closest friends there was a man called Duncan Robinson, who directed the British Arts Center, which was the center that had been formed out of Paul Mellon's own collection of British art. Linda and Duncan knew each other very well, and I got to know Duncan very well. Entirely by chance, Duncan, Paul Mellon, and I had all gone to the same Cambridge College as undergraduates (Britain is a very small world)—Clare College.

What is more, when Paul Mellon went to do a second BA at Clare (having first been an undergraduate at Yale), he studied history, and he attended the lectures of the then Regius Professor of Modern History, a man called George Macaulay Trevelyan, whose biography

I had just written. So I think my name came up as a result of these connections.

Moreover, I had also written a book called *The Decline and Fall of the British Aristocracy*, and one of the themes of that was the sale by impoverished British aristocrats of great works of art to American collectors, of whom Andrew Mellon was one.

All those bits of this jigsaw, I take it, fitted together; and so I was asked to write the life of Andrew Mellon for those reasons, in so far as I've been able to reconstruct the story. Since it was a kind of upside-down coda to *The Decline and Fall of the British Aristocracy*, it seemed to me that I would be out of my mind not to say yes. So I did it.

It was a marvellous project. Andrew Mellon was a very difficult man: a very shy, retiring man of few words, whom, after fifteen years of living with him, as it were, I didn't feel I knew any better than I did at the beginning. He lived an amazingly interesting life as this Pittsburgh banker and venture capitalist who created Koppers, Gulf Oil, Alcoa, Carborundum—he was really the man who transformed western Pennsylvania into the great industrial area that it was. Then he was Secretary of the Treasury. He was also a great art collector who created the National Gallery of Art in Washington. It was an extraordinary life, and to be invited to write it was an amazing fluke. I wouldn't have missed it for anything.

HB: Let me ask you a little bit about the art of writing biographies, in particular how that experience differs from narrative and other forms of history. You spoke just now about "living with" Andrew Mellon for fifteen years and not feeling that you necessarily knew him any better after all those years had past. That seems a difficult sort of experience to me. Are some historians more cut out for biography than others, you think? Do biographies have a near and dear role in your heart? Or are they just one form out of many?

DC: One of the things that I enjoy about being a historian—and one of the reasons why, although I have two marvellous publishers, I'm rather the despair of them—is that I never like to write the same book twice, or even to write the same sort of book twice. I like to do different sorts of subjects and devise an appropriate expositional structure for the sort of subject that I'm doing. Biography is one particular aspect of that more general issue.

It's also the case that one of the influential figures in my life as a historian was J. H. Plumb, whom I mentioned earlier. He is probably not as widely read now as he used to be, but when I was growing up he was another of these extraordinary figures (along with Briggs and Hobsbawm and all the rest of them) who was producing books of enormously high quality which reached a broad audience. Of course, the great—alas, unfinished—project of his writing life was the biography of Sir Robert Walpole, of which he wrote two volumes. I grew up with that, along with many other things, in the background. I was dimly aware, even when taking A levels in high school, that there was a kind of debate about whether or not historians should write biographies, and if biographies written by historians are the same as biographies written by professional biographers.

Nevertheless, I wasn't entirely sure that that was a very interesting issue. It seemed to me that biographies were something that I would want to have a try at as I matured, or tried to develop, into a professional historian.

I've now written three biographies: the biography of George Macaulay Trevelyan, the biography of Andrew Mellon, and the short biography of George V. I've also been appointed the new general editor of the *Oxford Dictionary of National Biography*.

So, it's an interesting subject for me, and certainly I've tried my hand at it—but, again, in various different guises. The Trevelyan book was organized thematically. It didn't seem to me that the day-to-day substance of Trevelyan's life was particularly interesting. Most academics don't actually live very interesting lives. They might do interesting work, but they don't live interesting lives.

I was eager to draw attention to the nature of his work: the dominant themes that ran throughout his life as a historian, and how to some degree those engaged with his broader public work. That life, then, has a set of thematic chapters, each of which goes all the way through his life.

The Mellon book is a full-dress biography. It's very long. It depends on a huge array of archival resources, which I was able to get round because I had research assistants who could do some of the work. It proceeds very much chronologically, but because Mellon had so many themes to his life—his private life, his family life, the moneymaking, the bank, the businesses, the art collecting, the philanthropy, and the politics—within each chapter I had to structure the different themes to move the life forward year by year on a whole variety of different fronts.

The George V life is quite short—only 25000 words, five chapters of 5000 words each—which turns out to be exactly the right length for dealing with him.

In each of those cases the biographies were written to a slightly different remit, imposed by either the publisher or, in the case of Mellon, the Mellon Foundation.

They have come out as very different sorts of works. I enjoyed writing them all. I do think that historians write biographies differently from professional biographers, because I think we have a broader sense of context, a broader recognition that the historical process is not just driven forward by single individual figures.

HB: The "Great Man Theory".

DC: Yes. So, I think this gives us a better perspective on some of these individuals than professional biographers have. But certainly for me, writing those three books has been hugely interesting. Entirely by coincidence, all three of them were rather gruff, shy men—'barking shyness' is a phrase that would apply to all of them. I think it's high time I wrote about someone who laughed rather more and talked rather more.

HB: Do you have anyone in mind?

DC: I don't have anybody specifically on the stocks at the moment. I've written an awful lot of essays about Winston Churchill, about whom I love to write. Certainly he didn't do 'barking shyness', so that's a different mode altogether. He's enormous fun. I teach a junior seminar here at Princeton on "Churchill and Anglo-America", which seems to go well. One of these days I might end up writing a life of Churchill. There are lots and lots of them already, so one might want to ask, *"Is there any room for another one?"* but I think there might be. That is a subject that perhaps I'll get to one of these days.

I also have the idea of writing a book that would consist of a set of essays about British composers, focusing on Arthur Sullivan, Hubert Parry, Edward Elgar, Ralph Vaughan Williams, William Walton and Benjamin Britten.

I'm rather interested in the notion of looking at composers as historical personalities, not just as great men who compose great music (although that could be said of all of them), but where they came from, what their social origins were, what their education was, how they presented themselves as composers, how much money they made, what honours they got, and how far their work has remained in the repertoire since they died.

It would probably be called *Composers Without Music*. That might well be an absolute 'no no' for any publisher, but it seems to me a rather good subject. It might work.

So that's another thing that's somewhere down the road. One of the difficulties as you get older, of course, is that you reach the stage where you can think of at least ten books you'd like to write, but since writing books takes quite some time, the brutal truth is that that's not going to happen. At some point, one has to decide which ones to try to write—and hope to live long enough to write those—and which ones not.

Certainly, the Churchill idea is one that I suppose one day I might be drawn to. This book about composers is one that I'm especially drawn to, because, once again, it would be a wholly new sort of book for me to write and it would require a wholly new sort of expositional structure. In fact, I've done the Elgar essay ("Orchestrating His Own Life: Sir Edward Elgar as a historical personality" in *Elgar: An Anniversary Portrait*), which I did feel went rather well. So I might get to that one of these days.

Questions for Discussion:

1. Are you surprised to hear that there might be a difference between a "professional biographer" and a historian?

2. Would you be interested in a book entitled "Composers Without Music"? Why do you think that David suspects that such a title would be "a no-no for any publisher"?

III. The Undivided Past
The origins of a deliberately provocative venture

HB: Let's move to *The Undivided Past*, as promised. As a reader I had a sense that this was a book that represented a sense of frustration that you had long held in terms of the rather stereotypical Manichean treatment of 'us versus them' that exists at various different levels of society, from the man on the street to professional historians. Is that fair, or not?

DC: Yes, that is fair. It's a book totally unlike any other book I've written, which may be good or may be bad. Different people have different views on that. It came about in quite a complicated way. The immediate cause was an invitation to give the Trevelyan lectures at Cambridge. It's a hugely great honour to be asked to give those. It put me in very illustrious company, which I was very privileged, if slightly intimidated, to belong to.

Of course, I had written Trevelyan's life (*G.M. Trevelyan: A Life in History*), so it was a peculiarly agreeable thing to have been asked to do. The idea of those lectures is that you take on a big subject to reach a broad audience—which is what Trevelyan himself had done—and since that's what I like doing anyway, that was fine.

Richard Evans, who was then the Regius Professor of Modern History at Cambridge, and to whom I believe I owe the invitation, said to me, *"I want you to take on a big subject so that undergraduates will come and listen."* And I replied, *"Well then, what about religion, nation, class, gender, race, and civilization? How's that?"*

HB: "Is that big enough?"

DC: Right.

So that was, as it were, the proximate reason as to how I began; but you're right in your thought that in some sense it was a book that I'd been toying with for quite a while. Where it sits in the "Cannadine oeuvre", to the extent that that's a subject, is that it's the third book in a trilogy I never intended to write.

The first book in that trilogy is *Class in Britain* (1998), which—again—I was spurred on to write because I was invited to give a series of public lectures at Columbia when I was on the faculty there. *Class in Britain* was about the way in which perceptions of British social structure had shifted from a kind of Marxist view of class conflict to a rather different view on the part of academics. That had opened up a whole new set of ways of thinking about British social structure, not just in terms of 'us versus them' or upper-, middle-, and lower-classes, but also in terms of a much more elaborately graded hierarchy. In that book I played with those different ways of thinking about how people understood the British social structure across the 18th, 19th, and 20th centuries, and how historians had contributed to those three different models that I'd played around with.

Having written that book, I then wondered how it would be if I tried to take on what was becoming by the 1990s and 2000s a big issue in the professional historical world that I inhabited, investigating the connection between the history of Britain and the history of the British Empire. This suddenly became a big issue and still is. The histories of Britain tended to ignore the Empire, while the histories of the Empire tended to take Britain for granted and just got on with whichever bit of the Empire they were concerned with.

I thought to myself, "Is there any scope for developing or extending—literally, geographically—what I'd written about in *Class in Britain* to something to do with the Empire?"

And so, *Ornamentalism: How the British Saw Their Empire* was the second instalment—although I never, as I said, thought I'd write the first instalment, let alone the second. *Ornamentalism*, in large part, was about the way in which this hierarchical model of British society was transported, or analogized, to the different parts of the world that the British either settled or came to rule.

It partly took off from Edward Said's book, *Orientalism*; and, of course, it's a play on those words in the title. Edward, who was a colleague at Columbia and whose work I much admired, had set up this dichotomy between the West and the East—hence "Orientalism"—built , in part, around racial categories; and while I was certainly not going to deny the existence of those racial categories and the animosities and antagonisms to which those certainly gave rise, I was also interested to explore the notions of, *How did the British Empire work? How did it function?* and *How did people see it?*

And it's clear that one of the ways in which it worked and functioned and people saw it, was as this rather elaborately-graded social hierarchy, either exported from Britain or analogized in the countries of rule in the Empire. And then there was a huge amount of dressing up and flummery, which somehow brought this alive and made it real.

One of the influences on that book was Clifford Geertz, the famed anthropologist at the Institute for Advanced Study at Princeton, who wrote a lot about the ceremonial, not just as an alternative to power but as a version of power. There is a lot of Cliff in that book.

So that was the second book. And then I thought that maybe this should be pursued a bit further. I've talked about class and I've talked a bit about race (although not much, and probably not enough, in *Ornamentalism*). Then I began to think about this whole notion of these collective categories, of which class was certainly one and race was certainly another. There was religion to add to that, and there was certainly gender. Then, of course, in the aftermath of 9/11, there was Huntington and *The Clash of Civilizations.*

So, in a way that, I must repeat, was almost entirely unforeseen and unpremeditated, there gradually came into my mind a notion of thinking about these different categories of collective identity and collective antagonism: religion, nation, class, gender, race and civilization.

I thought it would be interesting to have a try and looking at those side by side in a way that I wasn't aware that any historian had ever done, and to see what the claims were that historians made about these categories of analysis of the past and the use to which these categories had been put by political actors across the centuries.

I was beginning to think about this set of issues when the invitation came to give the Trevelyan lectures, an invitation with the particular suggestion that I should take on a big subject. So my first go on that set of issues was at the Trevelyan lectures.

They were fairly crude and schematic because I really hadn't written anything until the lecture invitation came. It was thus a chance to try out some very preliminary ideas, and the audience was very tolerant and sympathetic, but the book as it's finally emerged doesn't bare much relation to the lectures as given, except that it is about the categories that I've described. It has those six chapters, topped and tailed with an introduction and conclusion.

The general argument remains the one that I advanced in the lectures, which is to say that seeing the world in terms of these conflicts of 'us and them'—whether it's religion, nation, class, gender, race or civilization—is undeniably one of the ways in which we *have* seen the world in the past, one of the ways in which the world worked or didn't work in the past, and it's certainly the way we are constantly *invited* to look at the world today by politicians, pundits, and so on.

But the case I wanted to make was that that may all be true but there is another way of thinking about the world, which is these conversations across these allegedly impermeable boundaries of identity, which drew on the work of people like Anthony Appiah and Amartya Sen. That's really what the book was about and it's what the lectures were about.

And so it ended up finishing off, as it were, a trilogy that I'd never meant to write.

Questions for Discussion:

1. Is looking at the world through the prism of "us vs. them" a natural part of human nature, or does it need to be reinforced by prevailing societal influences?

2. What role does the media play in reinforcing divisive stereotypes that have little historical basis?

IV. Transcending Parochialism
The value of history

HB: One of the things that's interesting for me as a reader is that this is not so much a prescription. There are many people who urge us to see beyond our differences, to engage in fruitful communication with others, to recognize that we're not as different from others as we might like to believe we are. But yours is not a prescriptive philosophical work. It's not a moral work. It's a historical work.

It seems to me that what you're really doing is pointing out that, notwithstanding our collective sense that these impermeable divisions have always existed and have always played a key role in history, if one looks closely and carefully enough, one also sees ample evidence of trends going in a rather different direction.

That is, if we look at each one of the topics that you examine—be it race or nationalism or religion or what have you—there is a plethora of examples of those who have collaborated, who have demonstrated a willingness to compromise, who have showed considerable understanding of a broader perspective.

Again, these are *historical* arguments; and I think that's missing in the modern context, certainly to the man on the street who picks up the newspaper and who constantly hears this rhetoric of 'the clash of civilizations', this notion of 'us versus them'. Personally, I think that's a very valuable counterpoint to put out, again, from a historical perspective.

I hope that we'll have a chance to talk a little bit about possible prescriptive elements—what one can do with all of that, exactly—in a moment, but I think it's worth pointing out at the outset that for many of us, myself most definitely included, it's important to simply be presented with this argument, to be forced to grapple with a view that, historically, it's simply not true that dividing the world into these antagonistic categories has always been the case.

Many of us unthinkingly believe that this knee-jerk, Manichean tendency is an inevitable aspect of the human condition. So when you say, for example, "Let's look at how the Romans treated religious differences—let's look at how tolerant and practical they were," it makes you think. It's important to be reminded of this. Not everybody reads Gibbon as closely (or as regularly, I suspect) as you do.

DC: Well, that's certainly one of the things that I try to do in the book. In a sense, of course, it's a very derivative book in that there's no original research in it; I'm skating on a lot of terribly thin ice and covering large areas of human history that I can claim to have no expertise in at all.

But certainly one of the things that I wanted to do was to draw out a lot of historical work—quite a lot of it rather recent historical work—which has explored, in different contexts and with reference to different categories, the sort of conversations across the boundaries of identity, which historians are becoming increasingly aware have occurred.

For instance, in an earlier time it was commonplace to present the period of religious wars from the Reformation through to the end of the Thirty Years' War as a time of constant religious confrontation between Protestants and Catholics. What a lot of the recent work has shown—I must repeat, it's not my area of expertise, but so I have been able to learn—is the extraordinary way in which, if you go down from the level of theological disputation or princes fighting each other in the name of one religion rather than another religion, and look at the way people, on the whole, were living out their lives, it wasn't on the basis of those antagonisms at all.

There were households in which the servants might be of a different religious faith from the people who employed them. The churches were used for a Catholic service and then for a Protestant service. There was a whole variety of interconnections in ways that previously we hadn't understood as much as I think we now do.

And therefore one of the things that the book tried to do is to report on the way in which historians—some historians, not all—have recently begun to see that the history of humanity is about the history of conversations and dialogue as much as it's about the history of antagonism and war.

HB: Indeed. Again, as a layperson, this leads us to conclude that what we may be led to believe is necessarily inevitable—that there will be these profound cultural clashes, that people have always focused on differences between various different characteristics—is, in fact, not only not inevitable, it's not even necessarily true if one looks carefully. Of course there have been many clashes. Of course much of human history can be interpreted in this particular way, and you're not denying that, but that's not to say that it's always been the case and it's not to say that it will necessarily be the case in the future.

Which brings me to another point. One of the things that I found myself reflecting upon while reading this book was the timeless question of, *What is history for anyway*?

One of the things you explicitly mention is that history can liberate us from our present-day views, our present-day experiences, our present-day biases, that we might not otherwise question. It's a means by which we can transcend the ordinary and place things in a broader context. That too seems to me to be a motivation for you writing this. Is that right?

DC: That's certainly true. Going back to the historians with whom I grew up—that's to say, those I was reading as I grew up—they were all historians who wrote for a broad public. It's always been a view of mine that history is part of public culture.

It is generated—not entirely, but in large part, these days—in university settings, and it's crucially important if, like me, you're a practicing historian, to know what your colleagues are thinking and what they are up to; I regard that as a very important part and privilege of being a professional historian.

But in the end, we don't just write for each other as fellow academics, we write to be engaged in and participants in a broader public culture. That seems to me to be a major part of what we're doing. And it's certainly the case that one of the motivations behind writing *The Undivided Past* was to put forward the argument that the constant invitation to see the world in terms of these warring collectivities who are, as it were, predestined to exist and to fight, is not the whole of the human story; and we deeply misunderstand the human story if we don't understand that.

Beyond that, when politicians and pundits and false profits stand up and say to us, *"The world is very simple, and I will tell you how simple it is and all we need to do to fix it,"* it seems to me that it's constantly the job of the historian to say in reply, *"No, the world is very complicated; and you disregard that complication, not only at your peril but probably at ours as well."* And part of the purpose of *The Undivided Past* was to say, the world may have, on occasions, been built around simple animosities, but much of the time it wasn't and we need to understand that.

More broadly still than that, I think that the purpose of studying history, the purpose of writing history, and the purpose of reading history, is indeed to try to get ourselves *outside* ourselves. It seems to me that history is the most powerful antidote to the geographical parochialism—which assumes the only place is here—and the temporal parochialism, which assumes the only time is now.

Well, actually, an awful lot of people are living lives now very different from ours in other parts of the world and we ought to take notice of that. And, actually, most of humanity has had very different assumptions about how to live their lives than we have now.

In ten millennia's time, I wonder what people will make of us. I don't know how well we'll be thought to have done. I think it's very important for a historian to have a sense of that—that this is how we're living our lives *now* but in other places now, and in other times *then*, other people—maybe as decent as us, maybe more decent than us—have had different views and lived their lives differently.

I think that one of the purposes of historians is to try to explain how other people in other places or other times may have had views which we now find completely unacceptable, but that they weren't necessarily any less decent than we are.

So, history is a huge antidote to parochialism. And, with respect to *The Undivided Past*, one of the parochialisms that I'm targeting in that book is the parochialism that assumes that the way to understand all of the world is through these simple Manichean, binary, antagonistic categories, which seems to me simply not good enough.

Questions for Discussion:

1. Do you believe that professional historians are, to some extent, morally compelled to at least sometimes write for an audience bigger than their own professional colleagues?

2. Is the value of history as David describes in this chapter sufficiently imbued in our educational systems? If not, how might it be improved?

V. Categorical Examinations
The utility of boxes

HB: As you point out, one issue that arises by looking at six categories simultaneously is a logical one: it's logically impossible to imagine that the world can be divided into six pre-eminent factors for historical understanding and interpretation. It's conceivable that one of them can reign supreme, but that's about it.

DC: And, in fact, as I show in the book, they *all* make that claim, which was part of the attraction (or the challenge) of writing the book: placing these six identities—religion, nation, class, gender, race and civilization—side by side to try to see what claims were made on behalf of each of these.

Unsurprisingly, perhaps, it turned out that each of them made totalizing claims for the pre-eminence of this one single identity of the conflicts arising out of those identities and of that as being the motive power that drove the historical process forward. So, for example, one hears, "Religion is the most important identity which divides people and drives the historical process forward," together with similar claims made for each of the other five. Self-evidently, they couldn't all be right.

My own sense was that probably *none* of them were right in those extravagant claims that they made, even though for most of us of course it's the case that, since we are people of multiple identities—having a religion, carrying a passport, having some sort of social- and occupational-determined identity, having a certain sort of skin colour, a certain gender, and maybe even signing up to a civilization—these are all often significant elements in identities. But to elevate the claim of any single one of those above all others to be the most important thing about individual identity, collective behaviour, and the antagonistic processes which are assumed to drive the historical process forward seems to me to be a grotesque oversimplification. And part of the purpose of the book was just to lay all that out.

HB: Another point that occurred to me as I was reading is that there is often an assumption made by those advocating the pre-eminence of one particular categorization scheme that these categories themselves (or at least their favourite one) are fixed in time. But of course that's not the case either: Aristotle's notion of women and gender differences, for example, is strikingly different to what we think of today.

DC: Indeed.

HB: Similarly, the word 'race' seems to have changed enormously over time. Correct me if I'm wrong, but my sense is that 150 years ago or so, there was broad-based agreement on what race was really all about. Whereas today, I would guess that most people of a scientific disposition would say that it's an incoherent expression that doesn't really mean anything other than, perhaps, a way of self-identifying with others based upon, for the most part, relatively superficial and, when you come right down to it, fairly meaningless characteristics (like skin colour).

Put another way, it's very hard when you look at the word 'race' to get a proper scientific understanding of what we're even talking about. Where can "race" be found, exactly, in DNA? So the assumption that these are everlasting categorization schemes is, it seems to me, flawed in itself.

DC: Indeed, I think that's right. And obviously what we understand by 'religion', or what we understand by 'different religions', for example, has hugely changed and evolved over time. Many people now would suppose, to move on to the next of my six categories, that the nation-state is the kind of primordial, perennial and perpetual mode of human organization, but, in fact, if one surveys (albeit from a very high level) most of human history—as John Darwin wrote in his book *After Tamerlane*—the default mode of human organization has been empire, not the nation-state.

A world of more than a hundred nation-states—which is the world we inhabit now—is a creation of the last fifty years or so. It simply didn't exist in that form before. Many of the countries that are called nation-states are so different in their scope, their scale, their history, their sense of identity, their capacity to function, that to call them all nation-states is, itself, pretty strange.

The United States is a nation-state? Well, actually, it's a land-based empire—quite a successful one, but not really a nation in the sense that France or Germany are. North Sudan? South Sudan? What sort of a nation-state are those? India? Bangladesh? Pakistan? How did they come into being? What are they based on?

The whole notion that you can, as it were, pile each state side by side and say, *"There are a hundred of these and they are all fundamentally the same,"* seems to me to be simply wrong; and anybody who thinks this is normally the way that humanity has organized itself is also wrong.

So we have to be quite sceptical about these categories, these identities. The claims that are made on their behalf are often grossly exaggerated by those who feel themselves strongly associated with one in particular. And part of the purpose of the book was to draw attention to that.

HB: From my perspective as a reader, it seems that you had two different audiences in mind here, two different targets, as it were. On the one hand, there was the general public writ large: the media, the pundits and all of that: pushing back, as we've already discussed, at their rather trite phrases and interpretations of contemporary events in terms of these inevitable, impermeable boundaries which are actually misrepresentative of many aspects of our historical understanding.

But there is another point that I picked up on (perhaps wrongly). My sense was that you were also addressing the broader professional historical community, whom you feel might also sometimes be guilty of focusing too much on our differences, admittedly for different reasons. Is that right? Or am I somehow completely off base here?

DC: No, you're not. It is certainly true that there was a motivation to try to make some contribution to a broader public conversation about how politicians, religious leaders, journalists, and commentators invite us to understand the world. That was certainly part of the purpose of the book, and it's gratifying that I do get emails from people all around the world—not huge numbers, but sufficient numbers for it to be gratifying—saying they've read the book and it does help them make sense of things in a way that they aren't very often invited to do when they watch television or read the newspapers. That was part of what I tried to do; and in a very, very minor way, I think it's had some impact.

But it's also true that there's a kind of scholarly engagement with the book, a scholarly agenda to the book, partly trying to bring to public notice a lot of the recent work that has been done by some historians discussing these conversations across the boundaries of identity, but also taking issue with some other historians for whom the way to approach the past is through a single category of identity, which assumes a model of conflict.

I've lived long enough to see social history, gender history, cultural history—where many practitioners of those disciplines, especially in the early stages, were embracing those models while claiming that their approach to the past is the most important one that you need to understand above any other, that the identity they want to look at is more important than any other category, and that the way to understand the identity is that it's built around conflict.

I, of course, want to concede without a moment's hesitation that social history, cultural history, gender history, the history of race have hugely enriched our understanding of the complex and many-textured raiments of the past, and I count myself very lucky to have lived through this astonishingly fertile period in historical scholarship when that's been going on. But I think the danger is that if you adopt these approaches to the past built around one identificational construct—

HB:—which is pre-eminent—

DC: —which is pre-eminent. Then you tend to oversimplify the complicated nature of the historical process, because there's a lot of other things going on besides that. And you tend to make inflated claims for the particular identity you're looking at; and, therefore, you also tend to occlude those many aspects of the human experience, which are not built around notions of difference.

To offer a kind of crass example of that, there are a lot of people in the academy to this day who think that the essential route to the past is the secular trinity of class, gender, and race, and that's what you have to focus on because that will help you understand the things that are worth understanding about the past.

Well, I'm far from denying that those things are important—and, indeed, I've certainly written quite a lot about different people in different classes—but there is clearly an awful lot else going on in the human past that those things don't explain.

To put it in a crass and, as it were, recent mode: I'm not sure that class, gender, and race help us understand 9/11, but 9/11 is actually quite important. So, maybe we need to think a bit more about appropriate methodologies for the historical problems we want to address in order to try to work out what combination of the many broad and growing approaches to the past are most going to help us understand whatever it is we're trying to understand.

Whereas, if you start off by saying, *"The nation-state is the most important category to investigate..."*, *"Race is the most important category to investigate..."*, *"Gender is the most important category to investigate..."*, then you've already occluded many aspects of the human experience that are surely going to be relevant, even if you do want to understand the nation, or race, or class. That's, in a sense, where the book is coming from.

And in so far as there was a major academic influence behind that set of issues of the book, it came from reading a marvellous book, by my Princeton colleague, Dan Rodgers, called, which looked at several (not all) of the categories that I was playing with, and at the ways in which very strong claims had been made about their explanatory capacity and their totalizing encompassing of the human experience—in particular class, gender, and race.

In his book, Dan investigated the advent of those claims in the 1960s, 70s, and 80s, and then the gradual abandonment of those claims in light of the fact that more and more historical evidence came out, which suggested that the most extravagant claims were simply not true while, of course, accepting (as I myself do) that nevertheless, to say we ought to be aware of class, or gender, or race is, of course, very important.

HB: It has explanatory power, but it's not the only filter through which one should be looking.

DC: Yes.

Questions for Discussion:

1. What do you think David means when he says that the United States is "really a land-based empire that is not really a nation in the sense that France or Germany is"?

2. Is history more susceptible to the winds of academic fashion than other disciplines?

VI. Historical Broadening
Changing practices

HB: Is this view, broadly speaking, gaining currency? Are more historians now sympathetic to the view that we should be casting our net more widely, that as we look through these many different filters we shouldn't be raising any one of them to some pre-eminent level? Is that changing?

DC: I think it's changing a bit. Again, there are still those who think that "class, gender and race" is what you need to do and you don't need to do anything else, but I think they're a diminishing group of people.

There seems to be a growing awareness of the fact that the past now seems a much more complicated place than it did when I was setting out forty years ago, because so many more new approaches to the past have been adumbrated and practiced in that period.

The way the historical profession seems to work is that, every ten or fifteen years or so, someone comes up with a new approach to the past that begins by saying, *"This is what you've got to understand if you're to understand anything,"* which, sooner or later, merges rather more broadly and less stridently into a broader sense of how complex the historical process is. I think, on the whole, that's pretty much where we are and where we're headed now, but assimilating all these different approaches is a big job.

Another point I tried to make in the book—I don't think as successfully as I should have done—is to urge my colleagues that we need to engage much more with what's going on nowadays in a whole variety of relatively new scientific disciplines. I'm thinking here of the genome project in particular, but more generally a whole variety of work that's done on the nature of the brain, together with issues such as, *Does skin colour tell you anything, really, about how people are?*

There's been a big impulse, I think, over the past twenty or thirty years that is still very flourishing, on the part of certain scientific subjects, to start asking, *What does it mean to be human and what is human identity?* both in terms of how the brain works and in terms of how the body looks and functions.

And, of course, what the genome project shows is that claiming huge differences on the basis of skin colour is **simply not a scientifically sustainable position at all**. It seems to me that there is a lot of work from psychology and physiology about what it is to be human and what human identities are that I don't think historians are engaging enough with. I certainly make no claim to have engaged with it remotely adequately myself in writing this book.

I think there is still a temptation to say, "We should engage with Marx", or, "We should engage with Max Weber," or, "We should engage with Germaine Greer," or whoever it might be. I'm not against doing any of those things, and I do that in my own work, but I think the big conversation that we are not having enough of is—

HB: —with neuroscientists and geneticists.

DC: Yes. Exactly so. That is a conversation that historians definitely ought to be engaged in. I suppose part of what I tried to do in the book—but from an inadequate basis of knowledge on my part and therefore inadequately advocated—was to urge that we historians really need to get in on that conversation.

HB: Are geneticists and neuroscientists doing their bit? Let me take a specific example. Here we are at Princeton. Do you have opportunities to engage in any sort of systematic way with experts in cognitive science, say? Are there ample opportunities, or sufficient opportunities—or, for that matter, *any* opportunities for you to engage with them in a regular fashion here at Princeton?

DC: There is some scope for that. Princeton is a very remarkable university, because it is extremely good and it focuses a lot on undergraduate teaching. Compared to Harvard or Yale, Princeton is quite a small place, so it is actually easier to interact with faculty here, because there are fewer of them. There are quite a lot of opportunities for that, but I think there ought to be more.

I think that the conversation between the humanities and the sciences—I don't want to dwell too long on C.P. Snow and his *Two Cultures*—but I think that there is probably more scope for that conversation now than there has ever been before in my lifetime. In the old days, "The Two Cultures" meant that an educated person ought to know not just about whether Alfred burnt the cakes, but what the Second Law of Thermodynamics is—in other words, a broader definition of what an educated person needs to know.

But I think that the agenda, the arena of conversation now, isn't so much that we ought to know all these things because we ought to be well-rounded figures—although no doubt that's true as well—

HB: It's that they're directly relevant.

DC: Yes. It's that they are directly relevant, and there's a conversation to be had. I don't think enough of that is happening. I got interested in this when I ran the Institute of Historical Research in London. That's another influence on this book, which I suppose I only retrospectively became aware of. I put on a series of seminars about what it meant to be human, bringing in people from a wide variety of disciplines. I suppose that also sparked off this interest. But I don't think enough of us historians are aware that that's the sort of conversation we really ought to be involved in now.

Historians have "done", as it were, Marx; and they've "done" sociology; and they've "done" anthropology. They've been involved in conversations and got insights from those cognate disciplines. I'm all for that—and, indeed, in my own work I've done some of that too—but we're not so brave or venturesome as to have these conversations with people such as neuroscientists, which I think we probably ought to have.

I suppose all historians probably do have a model of what they think humanity is. I'm hoping you won't press me to tell you what mine is because I don't really know, but I suppose we all have a kind of assumption that humanity has always been the same and that we just behave the way we do. But that's not very rigorous, really—indeed, it's not rigorous at all—and maybe we need to be thinking about that a bit more. Maybe we do need to have conversations with a whole variety of people in the scientific community, not necessarily to take on board entirely what they're saying—we probably won't even understand quite a bit of what they're saying—but I think there is a conversation to be had. And since I'm a strong believer in conversations, this is another one I think we really ought to be involved in.

HB: It seems to me that even asking the question of what it means to be human forces one to take a somewhat different approach to historical research. For instance, there's been a fair amount of development over the last decade or two with respect to the notion of global history.

You mentioned earlier the benefit that a historical perspective naturally brings, enabling us to go beyond the 'here' and the 'now' and take a deeper, broader view of human behaviour and the human condition. Global history seems a natural sort of progression of this.

Is that gaining currency, first of all? Is this belief that it's important to take a globalized approach to history, for the very reasons that you enunciated just now, gaining favour?

DC: Yes, I think it is. It's certainly the case that global history and world history have become the leading sectors of historical inquiry in the last ten or fifteen years in a way that earlier on in my professional lifetime social history, cultural history, gender history and the history of race, were.

It's certainly true that that's where we are. It's certainly true as well in this department, where there are some extremely distinguished practitioners of global history, and we give quite a lot of attention to that both at an undergraduate level and at a graduate level. I think it's also true that there is some awareness, in the aftermath of 9/11, the financial crash of 2008, AIDS and—dare one say it?—Ebola, that we do now live in an extraordinarily globalized world, in which something happens on one continent and within a microsecond it has an impact on another. That encourages us to try to look back to what the earlier iterations or antecedents of that might have been, which is often a driving force behind historical inquiry.

So I do think that there is a push towards global history. I think it does have benefits. I think it does de-parochialize national histories, for instance; and if you do it the right way it de-parochializes gender histories, or histories of race, or histories of religion. I'm all for that for the reasons we talked about earlier.

I think it carries with it inevitable risks that it operates at such a high level of generalization that you might sometimes wonder if there is anything tough, or substantive, or hard here at all. And that can sometimes be a problem. How many global history books can the market bear?

Questions for Discussion:

1. Were you surprised at David's remarks about the need for more interaction between historians and neuroscientists? How common a view do you think this is amongst other historians? How common a view do you think that is amongst most neuroscientists?

2. Is it possible to pursue "global history" as rigorously as other historical approaches? Why or why not?

VII. What to Do, Part I
Advising presidents and educating Princetonians

HB: So there's the question of how many books can the market bear, but there's also the question of direct societal relevance. Let me return to the frame of reference of the guy on the street who might be listening to this discussion.

I imagine him thinking to himself, *Okay so I can't use race as the pre-eminent filter for historical understanding, I can't use class as the filter, I can't use religion as the filter.*

Twinned with this is the growing realization that what is being fed to me on CNN and in the newspapers is often a very simplistic, inappropriately combative, antagonistic, Manichean view—a 'Clash of Civilizations' view, or at least an overly simplified view of good guys and bad guys, and oppression and bitterness caused by gender, or class or religion or what have you.

So I can't use that explanatory framework anymore, because I now appreciate that the world is much more complicated than that and this approach is far too simplistic. But then I ask myself, *Well, can I say anything meaningful at all?* What do I have to hang on to if all I'm being told is that it's a lot more complicated than I had first appreciated: there are N different factors as N approaches a very, very large number, and it's all contingent upon time, or place, or what people had for breakfast, or whatever. If I'm in a situation where I can't make any synoptic judgment at all, then I don't really know what to do.

DC: Well, I think that's a very telling point. I constantly say to people, when I produce my homily that lots of people are in business to say the world is very simple and a historian's job is to say it's very complicated, that that's all very well, but suppose a desperate President Obama—and he'd have to be very desperate to be doing this—phoned me up and asked, *"What do I do about the Middle East?"*

If all I'd say in return would be, ringing my hands, *"It's all very complicated,"* he'd likely respond, *"Excuse me, I've got to have a policy here. And simply saying 'It's very complicated' is not a policy."*

I don't pretend to be indifferent to that point. I think it is a valid one, especially if you're in the position of President Obama.

More broadly, I suppose my reply to the question that you've posed in a slightly better way than I've answered it, would be the following: Of course it's true to say that 'everything is very complicated', which is just another version of "one damn thing after another isn't good enough".

So, here is my answer, which I'm afraid involves me rising to the supreme conceit of citing another example of what I try to do.

When I came to Princeton, the department was beginning to connect with, and get excited by, the prospects of global history. There were discussions about what I should lecture on, since we take undergraduate teaching very seriously here and I like lecturing to undergraduates anyway—I always find it enormous fun.

So I said, *"Well, at Columbia and at Cambridge, I taught British history."* And the reply was, *"That's fine, but actually we'd like something which could certainly allude to that, but which should look more fully at some issues of global history."*

I said, *"Alright. I've done quite a lot of work on monarchy and on empire. I've written a lot about the British Monarchy and I've written a lot about the British Empire, so maybe I could think about a lecture course which built on that, since 'monarchy' has been a global phenomenon and 'empire' has been a global phenomenon."*

Perhaps, I thought, I could devise a course that would be global in its geographical scope (because empires and monarchies have certainly existed globally), and which would, therefore, be genuinely global history, but would also avoid the hand-ringing, "It's all very complicated" and "one damn thing after another" because it would be organized around certain themes that were genuinely global.

In the end, I came up with a lecture course that is called *"Europe in the World: Monarchies, Nations, and Empires from 1776 to the Present Day."* I give this course at Princeton; I shall be giving it next semester. It gets a big audience. It goes from 1776 and 1789 to as near to the present day as we can realistically get; and it's concerned, at a general level, to make two points.

The first is that the way political units have organized themselves for most of human history has been monarchies, not republics.

Secondly, the way that political units have organized themselves for most of human history has been empires, not nations. For people who live in the United States of America—a nation-state as some think, a republic and a democracy—it's important to try to get them to see that this is a very unusual form of human organization, which has only existed in this country for two hundred years. It has only existed in some countries for a much shorter period of time than that, and in some countries to this day still doesn't exist at all.

So it's back to the business of trying to de-parochialize 'here' and 'now'. The way to do that is to begin with the American Revolution and to explain why that's so extraordinary, and then to look at the French Revolution, and then to look at the fact that throughout the 19th century most nations (and there weren't many) and most empires (there were a lot) were monarchies, not republics; and the French and the American examples were very much exceptions. It's only really since the second half of the 20th century that nation-states as republics and nation-states as democracies have become the widespread mode of organization.

That's an attempt to do global history because in the process I lecture about the United States, about Latin America, about Africa, about Russia, about China, but it's in pursuit of this broader point—since we are here to educate the gifted young, to provide them with some navigational equipment to make their way through life; that's what a liberal education is for—that there's no guarantee that in their lifetime the nation-state will remain the prevailing form of human organization, and whatever they may not like about the United States, it is a pretty remarkable and pretty unusual place.

So that's an attempt to do a certain sort of global history, with a certain kind of specificity, built around these notions of 'empire' and 'monarchy', and then subsequently of 'republics' and 'nation-states'.

Questions for Discussion:

1. Should professional historians be regularly advising heads of state? Are politicians more, or less, inclined to listen to historians now than they were 50 years ago?

2. Do you think that there will be more, or less "democratic nation-states" in existence fifty years from now than there are now?

VIII. What to Do, Part II
Harnessing technology

HB: So, that's a very telling and concrete example of how one can have something to grab on to if one happens to be a Princeton undergraduate. Now, let me ask you a question that you have no business being responsible to answer, but I'm going to ask anyway. You can probably see where this is going.

If you don't happen to have the good fortune of being a Princeton undergraduate and you are somebody out there in the broader world—it's a variant, I suppose, on the question of, what you'd say if President Obama would phone you up and ask for help—how might we be able to structure contemporary society, broadly defined, to be able to somehow not descend to the shallow, simplistic, media-driven stereotype?

These are, after all, a driving force in our contemporary democracy. This is how leaders get chosen. This is how policies actually do get made. How might it be possible for us to develop some sort of framework so that the average citizen can be more historically sophisticated? Not, perhaps, to the extent of a Princeton undergraduate, but still: how can we do a better job on a societal level at avoiding these trivial pitfalls of simplicity in terms of these Manichean dichotomies, which are so clearly not terribly productive and not even true for the most part?

How's that for a tough question?

DC: It's an extremely tough question; and you may not even know how tough it is. When I found myself at a party here at Princeton some time ago, I was in conversation with Neil Rudenstine who is an old friend, a very significant figure whom I much admire.

At some point in the conversation, Neil asked me what I was writing. Asking authors what they're writing is rather like asking people how they're doing: it's a deeply boring thing to do, and you really shouldn't do it.

Anyway, I told Neil, trotting out the usual thing about religion, nation, class, gender, race, and civilization. Neil is a very tolerant and long-suffering fellow. He turned to me and said, *"Yes, I'm really sympathetic to what you're trying to do in this book. I think it really needs saying. But I have to tell you, nobody will take any notice."*

That, in a sense, is his pithier version of the question you've just asked, because what Neil really meant was, *It would be nice if we could do something with that, but we don't seem to be in a world where we can.*

Well, if he can't come up with an answer to that, and you can't, I'm not sure that I can either. But I suppose that one goes back to the notion that this republic was founded on the idea of an educated citizenry. I take your point that not everybody can be lucky enough to come to Princeton. I take your point that the media, even parts of it that should know better, are interested in seeing the world in these binary terms—either presenting both points of view and assuming they're in conflict, or just presenting one of the points of view, which I think is a recent and particular trend in this country. These are not helpful developments. I think the notion of a serious commitment to try to be more aware of the complexities of the human condition, together with the degree of contact and the conversations across the boundaries of identity, is like good news in newspapers: it doesn't sell. Getting people to sign up for it as a commercial proposition is not easy.

HB: It's also hard. It's hard to do. It requires a lot of honesty and intellectual rigour. It's very easy to fall back on these stereotypes.

DC: Indeed. I suppose the area where I would like to think there might be some hope—I'm not sure there will be, but since I'm an optimist, let's go with hope—is that I think we are at the beginning of a huge revolution in higher education as a result of IT, as a result of the world of MOOCs, where it's going to be possible for a global audience to listen in to lectures previously confined to the lecture rooms of certain universities.

There are clearly lots of teething troubles with that, and maybe some of them will prove impossible to circumvent or surmount, but I sense that we are quite soon heading towards a world where a certain sort of higher education is going to become much cheaper than it's ever been before, and available to a much wider audience than it's ever been before. I think that's going to be a great revolution, which has barely started.

It would be exhilarating to hope that one of the consequences of that revolution might be a greater capacity to reach a broader audience talking about issues such as this and suggesting that there are other ways of seeing the world. Whether that will happen, I don't know.

A friend of mine once said, *"You must cultivate pessimism. There is no other way to indemnify yourself against misfortune."* But I don't agree with that. I think one should cultivate optimism in the belief that we can do better and ought to try to do better.

And I think this impending, just-begun revolution in higher education—which has certainly started in the US and the UK—does offer some hope of being able to reframe the kind of public discussion that goes on among people. And there will be far, far more of them, in a far greater span of the globe than before, who will have had the sort of education which will give them the means to participate in these sorts of conversations, and to have a rather more nuanced view of the world than too many small screens at the moment invite them to have.

HB: Is that optimistic view something which many, or at least some, of your colleagues share? Are you somewhat singular in your optimism?

DC: No, I don't make any claim to be singular in anything, really. I think that there is certainly a sense—and, again, it's something that's developing strongly here at Princeton—that the globalized world we're now in doesn't just mean that thinking about history as global history might be quite a good thing to be doing, but that in the globalized world we're now in, we have to devise forms of higher education (and the IT revolution has now enabled us to do it) which are, themselves, global in their outreach.

I don't, by that, mean that I'm eager to get rid of the campus university. I think what we're going to get is a much more varied set of higher educational offers, if I can put it that way. I do think that there is scope now for a global arena of higher education that will reach into parts of the world where higher education has not yet established itself.

HB: I understand that. I guess what I meant is that it's one thing to say that we need to be doing this because we have the technology, because our Provost tells us we have to be doing this, or our President tells us we have to be doing this, or what have you. As I'm sure you well appreciate, this sort of talk is all very trendy these days. There are university officials who proudly declare that they're doing MOOCs, and when you ask them why they're doing that, they'll start talking about branding, or tell you that they're doing a MOOC because, after all, MIT and Stanford do MOOCs.

That is one perspective.

But another perspective is what you were just describing in such an inspirational fashion: *My goodness, we have an opportunity to really take this educating mission seriously to a global level.* We now have the technology that not only enables us to disseminate these ideas to people who might never before have had the opportunity to partake of them, but also—getting back to the point you raised earlier—to find new ways of interacting amongst ourselves so that, say, neuroscientists could more easily have meaningful discussions with historians.

The first view seems to me to be something like, *This is the way the world is going, we have to sign on and maybe it's good or maybe it's not.*

The other view is an emphatically sanguine, emphatically optimistic view. That's what I meant by it seeming to me that you are quite optimistic about possibilities, and I was wondering how many of your colleagues share that virulent optimism or whether you are somewhat unique in that regard.

DC: Well, as I said before, I make no claim to be unique in this regard, or any other. I think you've set up a dichotomy, which—given the nature of *The Undivided Past*—I wish to break down. That is to say, I don't think Princeton is doing this because Stanford is doing it (although Stanford may be doing it because Princeton is doing it). But whatever the motivation, the fact remains that the big picture that drives what might be these slightly parochial university rivalries is the recognition of this possibility that you so eloquently sketched out. I don't think that these are at all incompatible. I think that a certain degree of rivalry between universities in pursuit of this greater goal will actually increase the likelihood of that goal being achieved. And it's certainly the case that there are quite a lot of people here in Princeton who are very excited by that possibility.

And while I think that unbridled optimism is probably irresponsible, I think that guarded optimism is a very good idea. Of course, from my perspective, if these extraordinary changes in higher education really do come to pass and develop, intensify, and expand in the way that I hope many of us would like them to do, then this sense of a "common humanity conversation" transcending the boundaries of these identities will be more hopeful and possible than ever before.

HB: Well said, sir. Anything you'd like to add?

DC: No, I think we've brought ourselves beautifully to an end.

HB: Well thank you very much, David. It's been wonderful chatting with you.

DC: My pleasure.

Questions for Discussion:

1. Do you believe that MOOCs have lived up to the potential that David describes in this chapter? Are you hopeful that they might in the future?

2. Has modern communications technology expanded or narrowed your exposure to new and different ideas over the past ten years?

Continuing the Conversation

Readers are encouraged to read David's book, *The Undivided Past: History Beyond our Differences*, which goes into considerable additional detail about many of the issues discussed here.

Ideas Roadshow Collections

Each Ideas Roadshow collection offers 5 separate expert conversations presented in an accessible and engaging format.

- *Conversations About Anthropology & Sociology*
- *Conversations About Astrophysics & Cosmology*
- *Conversations About Biology*
- *Conversations About History, Volume 1*
- *Conversations About History, Volume 2*
- *Conversations About History, Volume 3*
- *Conversations About Language & Culture*
- *Conversations About Law*
- *Conversations About Neuroscience*
- *Conversations About Philosophy, Volume 1*
- *Conversations About Philosophy, Volume 2*
- *Conversations About Physics, Volume 1*
- *Conversations About Physics, Volume 2*
- *Conversations About Politics*
- *Conversations About Psychology, Volume 1*
- *Conversations About Psychology, Volume 2*
- *Conversations About Religion*
- *Conversations About Social Psychology*
- *Conversations About The Environment*
- *Conversations About The History of Ideas*

All collections are available as both eBook and paperback.

www.ingramcontent.com/pod-product-compliance
Lightning Source LLC
Chambersburg PA
CBHW030903080526
44589CB00010B/119